Endorsements

"Information technology is ushering in a new era of human interactivity, one in which people around the world will be able to communicate in unprecedented ways. However, humans are just as complicated on both sides of a fiber optic cable as they are sitting together at a negotiating table. This book is an invaluable guide to this new era, marrying the technological savvy of David Coleman with the human insights of Stewart Levine. I recommend it to anyone curious about the new capabilities Web 2.0 is opening for human interaction and the ways we can use them to help us collaborate more effectively."
Colin Rule, Director of Trust and On Line Dispute Resolution, ebay

*"**Collaboration 2.0** is your secret weapon for successfully bringing people together in ways that maximize learning, communication, and results. The critical tools and insights will transform your organization and unleash innovation. Change it anyway you want!"*
Dr. Vicki Halsey, VP Ken Blanchard Companies and Author of The Hamster Revolution

"Collaboration 2.0 raises some important issues and challenges for us to rethink human communication at the intersection of people, process, and technology. Increasingly, people are using technology to connect up our best thinking, encourage new relationships, and stimulate innovative problem-solving that transcends culture and global boundaries, indeed making the world increasingly flat. I particularly like the introduction at the end to the role collaboration will play in helping us take on the challenges of envisioning a sustainable world that serves the needs of all people and ensures stewardship for the planet. It's time to have meaningful, courageous conversations on a scale not yet imagined that will help us create and live in the dream of a sustainable world."
G. Lee Salmon, Federal Consulting Group, Department of the Treasury

Also by Stewart Levine

Getting to Resolution: Turning Conflict Into Collaboration

The Book of Agreement: 10 Essential Elements for Getting the Results You Want

The Change Handbook, Chapter 52, The Cycle of Resolution

Also by David Coleman

Groupware: Technology and Applications

Groupware: Collaborative Strategies for Corporate LANs and Intranets

*We write because we have to say what we believe.
We discover what we believe because we write.
All else of writing is but a searching for form, a style,
a technique, to show those beliefs in an acceptable
artistic manner. When we succeed, our hearts are
on the stage to touch the hearts and minds of the
audiences. It is an awesome experience.*

- Unknown

Dedications

Stewart's Dedication:

For Susan Howard, for your support, caring, and all you taught me.

David's Dedication:

For Jennie Coleman: my wife, friend, and supportive partner who put up with my absence and preoccupation while I wrote this book.

Acknowledgements

We would like to thank those who contributed to the book.

From David:

First, I would like to thank Stewart (my co-author) and Mitchell (our publisher) for undertaking this project with me. We all collaborated well together, and I believe learned from each other.

Thanks to Near-Time for the use of their technology. Reid Conrad, Steve Dischinger, and Joel Bush provided us with an account during our research process. It also allowed us to collaborate on content and store various versions of the book while it was in process. We will also be offering a more dynamic, wiki-like form of the book through Near-Time in an online community at: http://collaborate.com/book.

Thanks to Rich Baker of Glance, an account that allowed us to easily share desktops. Using Glance 2.0, I could show Stewart (and others) what I meant and was able to share context as well as content. Through easy screen sharing, we were able to resolve many issues in true collaborative fashion without having the need to drive across the San Francisco Bay each time.

Thanks to the guys at Huddle for the use of their team space for the proofreading and content checking for this book.

A number of other collaboration technology vendors were most helpful in briefing us on their technology providing us with figures (graphics) and other material and contributing to my understanding of various behaviors and trends in the collaborative technologies arena.

I want to thank Mitchell Levy who has been working with us to get this timely book published in six months (rather than the long wait we have experienced working with other publishers). Mitchell also allowed us to experiment with developing online, dynamic, and collaborative versions of this book.

Thanks to my wife Jennie for gracing me with all the nights and weekends I needed to work on the book, which was time I could not spend with her.

Thanks to Ann Marcus, a Collaborative Strategies colleague, technology professional and my friend of 25 years, who collaborated on some of the research and presentations from which some of the material for this book was taken. Ann was also born with a red pen in her hand and did a lot of work in refining the content in the first part of this book.

Thanks to the guys at CommunityXperts—Dave Antila, Mike Dressler and Bob Sayle for their camaraderie and insight over last five years. Their experience, enthusiasm, and discussions about online communities and development environments have been both illuminating and very helpful.

Thanks to the people at New Ways of Working for their support (http://www.NewWoW.net). Their symposia over the years have provided a fascinating arena for discussion and understanding, where I have learned new ways of working. Some of the material for the final chapter came from the symposium Stewart and I attended in June of 2007 on environmental sustainability and new ways of working.

I thank Susan Mernit for her support, knowledge, and advice on social networks and collaboration in social media.

I appreciated the discussions with Karen Herzog and Richard Sachs of the Sophia's Garden Foundation. Karen's work on avatars was a great help for the book, and Richard's insights on creating objects in virtual worlds was most valuable. They are great friends and supporters of working collaboratively, and my interactions with them have both helped me learn and grow.

I would also like to thank my family for their continued love and support and for providing a context that enabled me to write this latest book.

From Stewart:

Special thanks to David, who created an identity around the website http://www.collaborate.com, for making this project seamless and effortless. I too share in your sense that "it was meant to be."

I find myself wanting to thank everyone who has ever contributed anything to my life, including my third grade teacher. Writing becomes a synthesis of all you know and all you want or need to say. So if your name does not appear here explicitly, please know that I acknowledge and appreciate the contribution(s) you have made to my life.

Thanks so much to John Maloney, who runs the Google group, and to Mitchell Levy for being so welcoming, for promoting and publishing this book, and for the leeway you have given us in the process. I especially want to thank Krista and Rosella of SBODN and Patricia Coate for introducing me to Mitchell.

I want to thank my partner Martha, who quickly let go of her resistance to my writing another book. She was so supportive during these past summer months when we might have been enjoying a bit of a respite together. You provide a wonderful foundation and a center that I am fortunate to have.

I want express a deep and abiding gratitude to my many friends from the Berrett-Koehler Publishers community. We have truly created a unique experience. First off, thanks to Steve Piersanti for inviting me in, supporting me, and publishing my first two books. The many authors I have met, the BK Author's Cooperative Board, and members, and especially to those with whom I have planned retreats and programs; you have become very dear to me. Thanks to Peggy Holman and Steve Cady, who selected the "Cycle of Resolution" for "The Change Handbook."

I want to acknowledge all of the virtual partners with whom I have worked with over the years to plan projects, events, and programs, large and small. I can now look back on how much has been produced virtually using collaborative tools of various kinds. I want to thank everyone I have worked virtually with over the years. I thank the supporters in the "Resolutionary Thinking" community (including the first two groups who went through the "Becoming a Resolutionary" program). Thanks to Jeff Aresty and Rob Pearlman for collaborating with me to create the eLearning program "ResolutionWorksOnline."

Special thanks to BJ Dorman and all my friends at CEO Space for their nurturance, for the opportunity to try new things and for allowing me to bask in the energy of a cooperative, collaborative environment.

Thanks to the American Management Association for the opportunity they provide. The phrase, "To Teach is to Learn Twice," sums up what you afford me. The same is true of the American Bar Association, including the eZine, for which I am privileged to write a column and the eLawyering task force on which I have served.

Final thanks must go to a family that, although distant, continues to provide an extraordinary foundation of love and support. You created for me a nurturing cocoon—a positive and inspirational context that has fostered my creative process.

David Coleman, October 10, 2007   *Stewart Levine, October 10, 2007*

A Message from Happy About®

Thank you for your purchase of this Happy About book. It is available online at http://happyabout.info/collaboration2.0.php or at other online and physical bookstores.

- Please contact us for quantity discounts at sales@happyabout.info
- If you want to be informed by e-mail of upcoming Happy About® books, please e-mail bookupdate@happyabout.info.

Happy About is interested in you if you are an author who would like to submit a non-fiction book proposal or a corporation that would like to have a book written for you. Please contact us by e-mail editorial@happyabout.info or phone (1-408-257-3000).

Other Happy About books available include:

- The Home Run Hitter's Guide to Fundraising:
  http://happyabout.info/homerun-fundraising.php
- Overcoming Inventoritis:
  http://happyabout.info/overcoming-inventoritis.php
- Happy About Online Networking:
  http://happyabout.info/onlinenetworking.php
- Confessions of a Resilient Entrepreneur:
  http://happyabout.info/confessions-entrepreneur.php
- The Business Rule Revolution:
  http://happyabout.info/business-rule-revolution.php
- Happy About Global Software Test Automation:
  http://happyabout.info/globalswtestautomation.php
- Happy About Joint Venturing:
  http://happyabout.info/jointventuring.php
- I'm on LinkedIn — Now What???
  http://happyabout.info/linkedinhelp.php
- Climbing the Ladder of Business Intelligence:
  Happy About Creating Excellence through Enabled Intuition
  http://happyabout.info/climbing-ladder.php
- The Emergence of The Relationship Economy:
  http://happyabout.info/RelationshipEconomy.php
- Rule #1: Stop Talking! A Guide to Listening:
  http://happyabout.info/listenerspress/stoptalking.php

C o n t e n t s

Figures

Tables

Foreword by Jessica Lipnack and Jeffrey Stamps

At the Seventh International Conference on Complex Systems in 2007, Barbara Jasny, Senior Editor at Science, cited a statistic that provoked a collective "wow" from the audience of complexity scientists. The current record for the largest number of collaborators submitting a paper to her prestigious journal? 350.

Jasny pointed to the truth that reigns in all domains these days: once the province of isolated geniuses, good work and breakthrough ideas congregate on the playground of those who can play well together. In our highly interconnected world, everything interacts with everything else and in order to understand—or accomplish—anything, we need to work together better. And, typically today, that means making use of innovative technologies and becoming adept at the human side of collaboration.

Not long ago, the word collaborator had a bad connotation in Europe, implying working with the forces of evil during World War II. But in a relatively short amount of time, collaboration has reclaimed its original meaning—"co-labor," to work together—and has become a popular term even in countries where it was anathema even a few decades ago.

Now in North America and South, in Europe, Africa, Asia, and the exquisite nations of Australia and New Zealand, to collaborate means that you know what you're doing. The trick is to do that supremely well.

When we were interviewing executives for our book Virtual Teams, nearly every conversation ended with a variation on the same idea: "You know, it's 90% people and 10% technology." This phrase has become something of a slogan for us and when a technologist has the capacity to speak from the people side, we always take notice.

We first met David Coleman a number of years ago at a conference on—take a guess—collaboration. He impressed us with his knowledge and his sense of humor, both vital to collaboration, and we've followed his work since, depending on him to be up on whatever was happening in that world. Invariably, he stresses that people are the ones using technology and that how and for what purposes they use it is far more important than the technology itself.

When we learned that David had teamed up with Stewart Levine to write the "next rev" of collaboration, we were intrigued and it took us approximately one second to agree to write this Foreword.

Stewart's grasp of the people side of the equation is comprehensive and practical. Good psychology, good people skills, and good common sense combine in his many ideas for how to make collaboration work.

The offerings in collaboration technology can appear like items in a supermarket, all the little cans bearing only tiny variations in ingredients to distinguish them. What David helps us see are the signs marking the aisles, pointing out the categories that we need to consider before making our choices, then applying expert stars to the ones he regards as best picks.

On the people side, Stewart enables us to zero in on the essence of collaboration. At the beginning, during the middle, and in the final analysis, collaboration is about communication. Prone to wanting to make our views known, we fail to listen. And listening across boundaries is the most difficult behavior of all. The borders that separate us stand in the way of our humanity and we need to dissolve them. "The ability to truly hear what others have to say is the most powerful form of communication," Stewart writes. We agree.

And though the word "business" appears in this book some 117 times, it is far more than a manual for business. As our scientist friends indicate, our world and indeed our future depend upon collaboration, which the authors make clear in their final pages. From global warming to alleviation of poverty to stemming the population explosion to reducing the threat of "weapons of mass effects," the human family needs to learn how to work together better very quickly and to become adept at using the best tools for doing so.

This book is your GPS for collaboration now and in the years to come. Open it anywhere and you'll learn something. Apply what you've learned and your work will become easier—and our hopes for the generations to come will soar.

Jessica Lipnack and Jeffrey Stamps, CEO and Chief Scientist respectively of NetAge, a consultancy that helps organizations work together better, and co-authors of many books, including **The Age of the Network and Virtual Teams**.

How This Book Came to Be

David's Story: This book came together so quickly that I truly believe it was meant to be. Everything just fell into place and we were able to develop it—from initial conversation to publication—in about 6-7 months. It has been an amazing process.

In April of 2007, I was walking the Web 2.0 Expo show floor one last time when I met Mitchell Levy, the CEO of HappyAbout Publishing. I mentioned to Mitchell that I was an industry analyst focused on collaboration technologies. We exchanged business cards and he asked if I had ever written a book. In fact, I had previously written two books on Groupware with Prentice Hall in the '90's. I then ranted about how the publishing industry is still stuck in the 1800's—with antiquated processes and technologies—and described how I had fought with my last publisher for the electronic rights to my last book even though the publisher had no idea what to do with those rights.

Mitchell wasn't fazed. He asked if I would consider doing a book on collaboration. I explained that it would have to be on *Collaboration 2.0* since I already had a lot of material for such a book. I told him I would consider it, if he could get the book out in less than a year, and that I could retain the electronic rights. Mitchell confidently said he could get it out in less than two months if we got him a clean copy and though he was hesitant to give me electronic rights outright, he was very willing to let me experiment with them. I was intrigued and told Mitchell I would get back to him.

I am a member of a Google Group (listserv) on Value Networks, to which many of my colleagues also belong. I monitor this group regularly and contribute occasionally. One of the group's members who responded to a post about collaboration was Stewart Levine. I was confident that if Stewart was a member of this online Group, to which he had been invited, he was most likely an expert in his area. Stewart and I exchanged several e-mails and agreed to meet a few weeks later for lunch.

At lunch, I found out that Stewart was a recovering lawyer and an expert in interpersonal communications, especially with regard to distributed teams. I told him about my idea for a book on Collaboration 2.0 and the holistic approach (people, process, and technology) I would take in addressing the issues. I asked if he would be willing to write the "people" and some of the "process" parts of the book. I would share the "process" part and I would write the "technology" part myself. Together, we could produce an amazing book, and one that is sorely needed. Stewart was delighted with the concept. He was particularly interested in joining me in a different kind of publishing experience. Over the next month, using several collaborative tools, we worked together on an outline and completed a book proposal.

By late May, we were both writing. Since we both had so much material already, our main focus was on collaborating on creating a coherent whole. Stewart and I worked diligently through the months of July and August. The second time we met face-to-face (F2F) was at the NewWoW conference on sustainability in San Jose.

By August, we had fully integrated the material and were sending each other new revisions on a weekly, and sometimes daily, basis. At the same time, Mitchell worked with us on creating the cover and the online Web site for the book.

We began discussions with Near-Time (based in North Carolina) on how to create an online community and wiki e-book. In this online community, we could add material we thought would provide additional value to interested readers. Then came the only painful part of the process, where Ann proofed the book for content, and Mitchell began insisting that we get permissions for all the figures and tables in the book, and that we needed to footnote all the links that were put into the text. This arduous process took about a month.

By October, we turned over the finished manuscript to Mitchell, who promised to have it out six to eight weeks! Stewart and I had only seen each other in person twice in this whole process (even though we only live a half hour apart) and we are living proof of the law of "Proximal Collaboration," which states that "when people are more than 50 feet apart, their likelihood of collaborating more than once a week is less than 10%."

Stewart Adds: This book truly was a collaborative effort. My hope is that the reader will appreciate the beauty of a book, written *about* collaboration that is the *product* of true collaboration! This book is a reflection of the creative potential of modern technology and processes that played a significant role in allowing us to work together so efficiently and pleasantly. That said, the critical component here was the human factor. It still comes down to people working together and the open and free lines of communication. David, myself, and others whose work we drew upon to create and then knit together the material is a rich snapshot of the state of the art of collaboration today—what we're calling Collaboration 2.0.

AUTHORS' NOTE: In telling our respective personal stories, we sometimes use "I" and sometimes "we." We apologize for any confusion this causes and trust that you will collaborate with us to make sense of it all.

Introduction

This book represents a first collaboration between David Coleman and Stewart Levine and examines collaboration from a holistic point of view—the technologies, processes, and people. David wrote Chapters 1 through 7 on collaboration technology and process; Stewart wrote Chapters 8 through 14 on process and people. David wrote Chapter 15, which is something of a summary of the ideas expressed in this book and applied to the Enterprise. Chapter 16 was written by both of us and reflects our views on the material we covered in the book as well as our hope for collaboration to provide one avenue to help reduce global warming and increase environmental sustainability. In this way, we made sure we covered the three elements that must come together to be successful in today's Web 2.0 enabled world.

We look first at technology, the most tangible aspect of collaboration. The majority of the examples and case studies in the book are taken from our experiences with global and geographically distributed enterprises. The goal of the book is to help people in these large organizations determine which processes might provide the greatest "collaborative leverage," and which technologies to apply to get the greatest benefit. When you couple technology and process with interpersonal styles, awareness, communication tools, and some conversational models that support "sustainable collaboration," you have a winning combination.

Chapter 1 examines what collaboration means, its definition, some of the benefits of collaboration, and how this book explores the subject. We also define "sustainable collaboration" and initiate a discussion about Stewart's Law of Agreement, which is a critical tool for distributed teams to function effectively. David then sets the context for an in-depth examination of collaboration technologies through a section called "The Technologies of Trust." We then move into an introduction of one class of collaboration tools called Virtual Team Space (VTS), which can also include collaborative portals and distributed project management (DPM) tools.

In Chapter 2, we look at 10 different trends in collaboration, some of which are driving the move to Collaboration 2.0. These 10 trends give the reader a more in-depth context for both the technologies and market for collaboration. David also looks at some of the market forces that are driving not only collaborative functionality, but also a large number of amazing mergers and acquisitions of companies in this space.

We explore the changing nature of the sales channels for collaboration technologies, and how buyers for these technologies have changed radically during the '90's. On the way, we explore "Unified Messaging," also called "Unified Communications," and what some of the major vendors are offering in this hot area right now.

We examine the importance of "presence," and some of the new applications that have the ability to detect and communicate the presence and status of users inside the application. Standardization of collaboration technologies is starting to take hold in the enterprise. We identify specific processes and industries that have "Collaborative Leverage." We look at the "self-service" sub-trend in the market and the applications that are becoming available to support this trend.

In Chapter 3, David uses his almost 20-year perspective to examine the overall evolution of electronic collaboration starting with the social or genetic imperative for humans to be part of the "virtual herd." We then look at the evolution of both interaction and communication technologies. Next, we take a 30,000-foot view of the first-, second- and third-order effects of collaboration technologies and how they impact not only your team, group, department, and enterprise, but society as a whole, both today and into the future, and the role they have played in various economic bubbles in the technology sector.

Chapter 4 looks at Collaboration 1.0 or working face-to-face, with a focus on content rather than the interaction between people. We then jump forward to look at some of the characteristics of Web 2.0 and Web 3.0, the Semantic Web. Finally we look at collaboration and security, discuss why they don't have to be antithetical, and give some examples and case studies.

In Chapter 5, we move on to Collaboration 2.0, the heart of the technology part of the book, where the collaboration environment is today, and how some of the newer collaborative applications support the characteristics of Web 2.0. We also look at the *9X Paradox*, or why it is so difficult for people to adopt new technology over something they already have. Finally, we look at the wicked problem of time coordination, especially scheduling people to be in meetings—both physical and virtual—and some of the new technologies that are being applied to solve this problem.

Chapter 6, called Collaboration 2.5, looks at avatars, virtual worlds, and 3-D collaborative environments. Here, David is starting to look at what the collaborative environments of the near future will look like. He goes into some detail on how to build an avatar (in Oddcast), and how to use a virtual coach in a 3-D collaborative environment. The examples for this come from a pro-bono project he has been involved in for the last year called "HICO" (Healing in Community Online) built by Sophia's Garden Foundation, as a prototype and an example of the kinds of communities these technologies can support.

The rest of this chapter is a survey of a wide variety of virtual worlds (including Second Life, There, Meez, and Gaia Online) as well as 3-D collaborative environments (such as Qwaq, Tixio and Wonderland). We then look at a virtual augmented environment (JFerret from AMI). The chapter ends by looking at social networks (another hot technology) and how they are starting to interact with virtual worlds.

Chapter 7 focuses a bit less on technology and more on people and process. Here we begin to examine some of the challenges that virtual teams face. We look at the seven types of virtual teams, some of the background and history of distributed teams, and then examine Social Network Analysis (SNA) and VNA (Value Network Analysis) methodologies that allow organizations to evaluate communication and collaboration patterns for optimization. The chapter ends with a section on online communities and some best practices based on experiences in working with this type of community over the last decade.

In Part II of this book, beginning with Chapter 8, we shift from examining technology to addressing the critical components of interpersonal communication and some of the challenges that arise there. This is where Stewart's expertise comes in and he is the author of Chapters 8-14.

In Chapter 9, Stewart discusses tools and levels of awareness essential to building an effective communication toolbox. Chapter 10 deals with the notion of "Resolutionary Thinking," a mindset that contributes to effective and sustainable collaboration, coordination, and cooperation. Chapter 11 is a reminder of the basic steps in forming teams and the stages they go through, whether co-located or virtual, and the value of a strong team.

Chapter 12 covers some fundamental truths about collaboration framed by what Stewart calls "The Laws and Principles of Agreement." Chapter 13 discusses techniques for the creation of a shared vision and a pathway to desired results embodied in "Agreements for Results." It introduces the 10 Essential Elements of these agreements and explains why it is essential to spend time at the beginning of projects getting clear about desired results, pathways to achieve them, promises of who will do what, metrics for assessing progress and concerns or fears about moving forward.

Chapter 14 introduces "The Cycle of Resolution," an efficient, effective interpersonal collaboration conversational protocol for getting back on track when differences cannot be reconciled and conflicts develop that prevent moving towards desired results.

David returns to write Chapter 15, in which he provides the key ingredients and necessary steps for implementing collaborative technologies as part of your "Organizational Operating System." This system serves as a guide to apply the technologies and interpersonal techniques discussed earlier in the book, and focuses on how to be successful within the enterprise through a holistic approach that uses "people, process, and technology."

Finally, Chapter 16 summarizes our observations, recommendations, and conclusions and provides a peek into the future. It is also has some material from a symposium we attended this summer about environmental sustainability (read Global Warming), and the role collaboration technologies can play in reducing this impending threat.

Appendix A lists resources for collaboration in a Web 2.0 world, including a brief description of each resource and a link to their web site.

Part I
Collaboration: Technology and Process

The goal of the overall book is to look at collaboration holistically, examining technology, process, people and their roles in successful collaboration. The book is divided into two parts, with the first part focusing on the most tangible aspects of collaboration: technology and process. This segment of the book examines the evolution of collaboration technologies as well as looking at the cutting edge of these technologies as aspects of Enterprise 2.0. The goal is to give the reader the technical and market background needed to understand the focus on process and people that Stewart presents in Part II of the book.

1 Introduction to Collaboration

"Those who do not learn from history are doomed to repeat it."—George Santayana

What is *collaboration*? It is a term that has found its way into the press, and, which has been spoken about at conferences on almost a weekly basis. However, what does collaboration really mean?

As part of our research and as industry analysts at Collaborative Strategies (CS), we track 1,000 tools and services that claim to have some flavor of collaborative functionality. However, it has become increasingly obvious, based on the degree of variation in these products and services, that "collaboration" does not mean the same thing to everyone.

There are a variety of definitions for collaboration:

- The art of discovering what neither of us could produce or invent on our own

- The source of all productivity

- The dance of working with others

- The joy of engaging in an "I/ thou" relationship

- The key that will unlock the solutions to global challenges like war, violence, poverty, racism, environmental degradation, and human rights abuses

- More than the sum of its parts

- Assertiveness and positive regard in action

- All of us are smarter than one of us

- 1 + 1 = >2

Further refinements that help to identify some of the key subsets and elements of collaboration include:

- **Synchronous Collaboration:** A computer-mediated interaction between two or more people that occurs within 5 seconds (e.g., an instant message)

- **Asynchronous Collaboration:** No time limit on the interaction (e.g., an e-mail or threaded discussion post)

- **Semi-synchronous Collaboration:** Interaction with intervals longer than 5 seconds but within some prescribed time frame (e.g., a webinar [real-time] that is recorded and saved for a day so those that missed it can see it)

- **Data:** Bits and bytes

- **Information:** Data put into context by a human to give it meaning

- **Learning:** The process of internalizing information, relating it to what we already know

- **Knowledge:** The application of information, either as action or communication

With the obligatory definitions out of the way, let us look at some of the benefits that collaboration can provide.

Benefits of Collaboration

There are four major benefits from collaboration:

1. Saving time or money (tangible)

2. Increasing quality (tangible...but less so)

3. Innovating and/or providing decision support (tangible, but less than quality)

4. Easing access to and interactions with subject-matter experts (intangible)

In any collaboration, people are the critical ingredient. None of the above benefits can be realized without people being willing to trust and share both the content and themselves. This is true for distributed project teams as well as for tiger teams dealing with a crisis. In the work CS has done over the last decade, we have found that distributed teams need to meet together in person first, and then again in person about every 6 months to keep the trust level high and the sharing effective.

In the next section, we will discuss why collaborations fall apart (from a people perspective) and introduce the idea of "sustainable collaboration" and a principle that is critical for collaboration: "The Law of Agreement."

Sustainable Collaboration and the Law of Agreement

One of the key reasons collaborations fall apart is that people working together do not spend enough time at the beginning of their collaboration creating a joint vision: defining what they want to accomplish and how they will accomplish it together. I call this creating "Agreements for Results."

The key premise on which "Agreements for Results" are based is The Law of Agreement[1] which says that

- All productivity and satisfaction in professional and personal relationships happens because we collaborate with others, and,

- All collaborations are embodied by an explicit or implicit agreement about what we are doing together.

Sustainable Collaboration is the ability to maintain productive working relationship for as long as people want to because the collaboration is held within the container of a clear "Agreement for Results." This container includes a process to quickly get back to collaboration when people are not effectively collaborating.

Collaboration typically breaks down because either all those involved have reached no agreement, or the agreement is ineffective. Invariably the solution for an unproductive collaboration is to put in place an *Agreement for Results*. Collaboration essentially is a function of an effective relationship. As we know, building effective relationships is very subjective.

Example

> *In the early 1980s, I was working for the old AT&T. The company was gearing up to move from a world where everyone waited for their marching orders from corporate headquarters into a new era, the post-divestiture world in which competition and entrepreneurship would reign supreme. I had a progressive manager at the time who was open to letting us push the edges of our new environment and evolving culture.*
>
> *By collaborating with our manager and a volunteer team, we were able to develop an innovative work style that resulted in the design of a new telecommunications application. Without waiting for corporate headquarters to tell us what to sell and how to sell it, the collateral to use and what to charge, we plunged ahead, creating both our process and our results as we moved forward. The team*

---

1. Stewart Levine, *The Book of Agreement* (San Francisco: Berrett-Koehler, 2002).

members were empowered by each other and the excitement that our collaboration generated. We called ourselves "The Mod Squad," after the popular TV show of that era, because our work style embodied this modern philosophy of collaboration and self-regulation.

We were so successful that senior management asked us to travel around the country and teach others what we were doing and how. As I think back, I remember the joy of collaborating, how productive we were, and how much fun it was to forge new territory.

Collaborating effectively is a holistic activity, especially on high-performance teams. It is personal, and sometimes intimate, requiring exquisite attention to the nuances of another's presence and personality and the ability to pick up subtle verbal and physical cues. It is not unlike dancing. In collaboration, one must pay attention to the whole of the project and the whole of the team. Anything less is mechanical, a going through of the motions of a process someone else set up, *check-listing* a set of activities asynchronously, rather than creating cohesively in the moment.

Because collaborations *are* so personal, it requires dedicated participation in a continuous feedback loop. Without this, true collaboration does not take place. Yes, you might be adding value to a desired outcome, but it is not one forged of an interdependent set of activities, reliant and affected by the actions of others. When everyone is fully responsible for the result, and innovation is required, the process must account for the whole.

In the next section of this chapter, David examines the myriad of collaboration technologies available today, and what some of the key factors might be in selecting one (or more) of these technologies for yourself, your group, your team, or your enterprise. Given the high touch of collaborative communication the application specific selection of the tools is a critical part of the success factor.

Technologies of Trust

With over 1,000 vendors on the "collaboration" bandwagon, it is difficult to know which technologies would be right for you and your organization. For instance, which vendors actually support collaborative functionality (rather than just hype) and what strategies do they have to aid you in the adoption of these applications across your enterprise or value network? The goal of this part of the chapter is to look at some of the key factors for selecting and implementing collaboration technologies successfully in the enterprise. However, we will revisit this theme in more detail in Chapter 15.

Remember the old advertising slogan, "I've fallen, and I can't get up!" It could just as well apply to the predicament of many collaboration vendors today. They have had great success in pilot projects, but cannot seem to get greater penetration of their technology or higher adoption rates in the enterprise, no matter how many new features they add.

Many of these vendors are slowly coming to realize that collaboration success is not really about features and functions, but rather about how well the technology integrates with and supports processes critical to the organization, *and how the organization manages its own systemic change process.* Yet many of these same vendors are unprepared to tackle this problem within their own professional service organizations. The best way to counteract these drawbacks is a holistic approach to collaboration.

When speaking about a holistic approach, there are three critical factors for success in collaboration (in order of importance):

- **People** (behaviors, attitudes, culture)

- **Process** (critical business processes with collaborative leverage)

- **Technology** (offers good user experience, integrated and connected to many data sources)

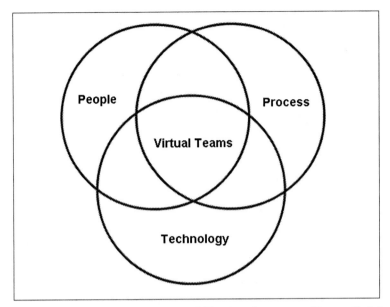

Figure 1: People, Process, and Technology are Essential for Successful Virtual Teams

For any type of collaborative behavior to occur, there must be some level of trust in place, either for the ongoing sharing of complex information, or the coordination of tasks over time. Yet collaboration technologies do not inherently engender the attitude or belief of trust. The critical role of technology is to support the interactions between people so that they can establish trust, which will then allow them to share and coordinate their work.

The key word here is *people*. When talking about the ongoing social interactions of two or more people, we are talking about relationships and we all know how challenging those can be.

A few years ago, I (Stewart) was presenting at a conference of CIO's of Major Law Firms and Law Departments. I was heartened and gratified to hear almost every presenter (tech types all) admit that it did not matter how good the technology was—if people could not communicate well, the best technology was not going to save them. I realized then that every technological implementation needed both a communication/trust/relationship building component and a change management element if the implementation was going to be successful.

The Pareto Principle—also known as the 80-20 Rule—states that, for many events, 80% of the effects come from 20% of the causes. This would suggest that 80% (or more) of the effort in collaboration has gone into the development of these enabling technologies; 20% (or less) has been focused on the relationships or interactions between people. Why? Because the software tools are tangible, and are what both vendors and CIOs are most familiar with and, in reality, are much easier to deal with than relationships. *Software code is much easier to change than people's behavior.*

Relationships, trust, behavior, and attitude are all "the soft stuff" and are not within the mindset of most software vendors and CIOs. If the collaboration strategy in the enterprise is left up to technology people, then technology is what you get. Often these "solutions" don't solve the real problem, and as a result they are often left unused or abandoned by the business units for which they were developed or purchased. They often reflect IT goals but don't really reflect critical processes or the culture of the team, department, or organization. So if the technology people are not dealing with this "soft stuff" whose responsibility is it?

To answer this question, let's address the notion of *collaborative pain* and the *real cost* associated with ineffective collaboration. Collaborative pain occurs when the lack of information sharing or coordination in a critical process slows down the cycle time sufficiently to create a serious problem for the process or project owner.

It is easy to see how the process or project owner, in effect, then has responsibility for the "soft stuff" of collaboration. Whoever has profit and loss responsibility—for the project, process, department, or coalition of which the process is a part—has this responsibility. This individual would be wise to take a holistic view of collaboration as success depends on their ability to address people, process, and technology issues simultaneously with the heaviest focus on people.

Collaboration is, we believe, primarily about people, about trust, and about the willingness to share information and work in a coordinated manner to achieve a common goal. This premise, which is the focus of Part II of this book, will establish how interpersonal skills are needed to effectively use many of the collaboration technologies we describe here in Part I.

Process, Process, Process

Processes in an organization provide a framework in which to engage in the trusted behavior of information sharing or coordinated work, or what we call "collaboration." One of the biggest benefits of collaboration is its ability to cut cycle time (although there are other benefits). Because the Internet has us all expecting events to happen faster, if not immediately, cycle time has become not only a critical competitive advantage but today, a bottom-line expectation. That expectation continues to increase as more and more technology becomes available in this Web 2.0 world. Combine this with the fact that processes and projects are getting more complex and distributed, and we have a challenging situation.

In the 90's, collaboration was primarily about working with colleagues within the corporate firewall. Today, it often means working with people inside and outside the organization (in your "value network") who have a wider spectrum of roles and relationships in this ecosystem that develops across and between organizations. All the old rules of process efficiency and optimization still apply however, but today they must be translated to work across organizations, which often mean creating a Virtual Team Space (VTS) that is driven by collaboration. What we mean by a VTS is a secure virtual space where process or project objects can be stored, discussed, modified, and searched.

Working with some Fortune 500 companies revealed that collaboration is most effective in dealing with process exceptions. A process exception is a behavioral action that falls outside the process norm. For example, most customers can get many of their questions answered by either reading the FAQ or talking to someone in first-line support. A process exception would be when an irate customer has not been satisfied from any of the standard processes and is moved up to second or third tier support. Often at these support levels not only do the support staff know more, but they will often work with each other (collaborate) to get an answer to the irate customer's question or issue.

Pareto's Law also applies here: Typically, 80% of focus and attention in a process is on the part that is successful, while only 20% is applied to process *exceptions*—the stuff that goes wrong. Just the opposite should happen, because, in reality, process exceptions take up 80% of your resources and are often the most cycle-time sensitive. Remember, that irate customers, if not satisfied will tell 10 others of their experience and there is no telling how much that will negatively impact your bottom line.

For example, not getting back to an irate customer with a good and timely solution can be extremely damaging. Or in a distributed new-product development team, if one of the team members from a partnering organization is not kept in the loop, that individual can often dramatically slow down the release of the new product.

So with this short discussion on both "people" and "process" we move on to the third factor in this triumvirate: "technology."

Is "Collaborative Technologies" an Oxymoron?

Initially, collaborative technologies were so complex, expensive, and difficult to use that they were, themselves, barriers to collaboration and got in the way of interactions for everyone but the most tech savvy. These technologies have advanced significantly over the past decade. Today, most collaborative tools help rather than hinder the social interactions inherent in collaboration. These interfaces—often browser-based—have become more standardized and intuitive, requiring little or no training. They support multiple media (audio, video, and data), are becoming less expensive (or in many cases free), and can integrate with a wide variety of content and object types (e-mail, multi-media, avatars, web pages, mashups of public and private data, etc.).

Marshall McLuhan, once referred to as the "Oracle of the Electronic Age", is perhaps best known for uttering the catch phrase: *The medium is the message.*[2] For collaboration technologies, the medium has frequently gotten in the way of the message. These technologies should add to and support people in the way they work most naturally, instead of demanding that people change their work behaviors to adapt to (the limitations of) the technology. Collaborative technologies should provide a common context or framework within which to interact.

This trend towards computers supporting human behaviors called "human-based computing" is a trend CS has been tracking for the past several years. This trend is the confluence of sophisticated and flexible hardware and software with faster connection speeds that finally creates support for people to work in a natural way, rather than bending their behavior around the system.

Today, the user of these tools has a much wider user experience, many of the tools require little learning, and if they are offered as a service, there is often little or no cost to set up and try them. Most of today's new tools, Collaboration 2.0 tools, are in sync with the tidal wave of user generated content that we are all drowning in, and they support many of the multimedia modalities demanded of collaboration today.

Collaboration technologies are beginning to support what we call "on-demand collaboration," where one can move fluidly and naturally from solo work to teamwork (asynchronously or in real time with team members or partners in other organizations). This is one of the holy grails of collaboration and we are almost there. On-demand collaboration could be seen as a subset of the "human-based computing trend" in that the ultimate goal of the software is to support people in their computer-mediated interactions.

CS research since the beginning of the millennium has shown the emergence of real-time collaboration (RTC) technologies that not only support IM/Chat but also support interactions in any or all of audio, video and data conferencing mediums. In addition, these tools are

---

2. Marshall McLuhan, *Understanding Media, The Extensions of Man* (Cambridge: The MIT Press, 1994).

browser-based, easy to use, and support both ad-hoc and planned events. These technologies are not yet where they need to be, but are rapidly heading in the right direction.

I (Stewart) can attest to the ease of use. Although I have been toting a lap-top since 1988, I am anything but tech savvy. Over the past few years, I have been able to navigate the use of webinar technology to deliver a twelve week virtual training program delivering the communication skills I will speak about in Part II of this book. The technology enabled a rich collaborative learning experience for people who were located all over the country. That said, they were all self-selected volunteers who wanted to learn and change.

However, the interactions of people often form a complex system, and collaboration is an emergent characteristic of those systems. That is, the system is complex and cannot be easily reduced to its component parts (usually people), and an emergent characteristic, like collaboration, springs from the plethora of interactions of the parts in that complex system and can't always be either predicted or managed.

As David mentioned earlier, the CIO's have been using these tools in their organizations, and have focused on the technology. In the future, there will be better predictability and management within the human conversational aspect of collaboration when we begin incorporating tutorials and especially designed communication protocols that require a certain kind of engagement.

Technologies for Collaboration

A crop of powerful tools for distributed-team communications are appearing by the dozen, each with a slightly different set of features, functions, or focus. VTS tools allow work groups to share project information, documents, and images mostly in an asynchronous way.

The most high-profile entries in this market come from the industry big guns: IBM's Lotus QuickPlace (now called Quickr) and Workplace, EMC/Documentum's eRoom, Microsoft's SharePoint Services. But there is a whole crop of new Web 2.0 tools that fit into the VTS space including:

- Jive's Clearspace
- Huddle
- Near-Time
- Teamworkzone
- Central Desktop
- Nexo
- Collanos Workplace
- OpenTeams

Enterprise Tools

VTS tools have been evolving over the past decade, but their exact point of arrival is a bit difficult to track, because the category of technologies has been known by a variety of names. *Portals*, for example, is the term used to describe doorways into internal, employee-facing *intranets* that aggregated key internal information and made it easy to access, though not all team members knew how or were permitted to post information to these internal resource sites.

As it became evident that working with external entities across the supply chain or with the customer base was of value to the organization, secure sites, called *extranets*, were developed that aggregated information for the group of internal and external participants on a project team. Getting to these sites, however, could be tricky if participants tried to login from a computer other than their own from a fixed location (often required a VPN [Virtual Private Network]). The latest iteration of VTS tools are wiki-based team spaces. These were designed to make it relatively easy for participants to access and modify shared material, and since many of them are offered as a service, the users often did not need IT involvement to get them up and running.

This is in contrast to many of the enterprise collaboration tools like IBM/Lotus Notes or Microsoft SharePoint and Exchange. These enterprise-sized applications require IT department involvement to install, configure, and maintain these applications. They are designed to manage almost every imaginable need of collaborative teams—whether separated by cubicle walls or national borders, within and between organizations.

Intel's SharePoint installation, for example, serves Intel's 80,000 employees worldwide as well and extends to many thousands of external consultants, customers, and others entities in its supply chain, with gigabytes of multi-level security-protected information shared across the world.

These enterprise-based virtual team tools contrast sharply with Web 2.0-based applications, many coming from startups, that have low overhead, a low initial investment of money, take almost no time to learn, can serve small to large teams, and may even focus on a specific vertical or horizontal niche. Often these tools can be used for smaller applications and can be under the control of the user rather than IT.

A few such web-based applications include CoCreate's OneSpace, for collaborative product engineering and development; Autodesk's Constructware, for the construction industry; and Synchris' Privia for collaboration in developing government contracts. For small vendors, specialization is a key differentiator in a market dominated by the likes of IBM, Microsoft, and Cisco with products designed to serve the masses. But serving the masses is Web 1.0, Web 2.0 is focused on serving the individual or small group and dealing with the "long tail" as it is called.

All of these terms (VTS, DPM, etc.) refer, in a broad or specific way, to a virtual place for those working on common issues to "come together" electronically to share information. They often take the place of a physical teamwork space, offer secure persistent storage for actively shared materials, and provide a log of who said what and when, or who touched what object, and when or what they did to it. Since everyone must come to the common space, it would be easy to provide a communication tutorial that goes way beyond how to use the technology. The people aspect is about "how to use the technology tools more effectively."

Typically, VTS tools have a core set of features, which include asynchronous communication (threaded discussions) and storage for various types and versions of shared documents such as schedules, drawings, photos, specifications, bills of materials, proposals, and so forth. They usually include simple document management (with check-in/check-out and version control) and often integrate with some sort of real-time tool like IM/Chat or web conferencing. Beyond that, they may include options from a growing list of possible features.

Here is a listing of the product categories that fall under into the VTS tool category; they include both Web 1.0 and 2.0 tools.

- Discussion/Bulletin boards (WebBoard, PhpBB)

- Content/Document Management (Vignette Collaboration, ShareMethods)

- Distributed Project Management (DPM) tools (PlanView, Projity, Clarizen, eProject, CopperProject)

- E-rooms, team rooms and e-collaboration tools (e-Room, Near-Time)

- Groupware (IBM/Lotus Notes, Lotus Domino, WebSphere Portal and IBM Workplace)

- Intranets/extranets (Intranets.com now WebEx WebOffice [now Cisco], Intranet Connections.com)

- Knowledge Management (Knexa, KnowAb, Tacit)

- Online Community tools/spaces (Yahoo or Google Groups, Q2Learning, iCohere, Dolphin 6)

- Portals (Plumtree [now BEA], IBM WebSphere)

- Wikis (GroveSite, JotSpot [now Google], SocialText)

Significant boosts in broadband adoption and the growing use of mobile platforms for information sharing have made the use of VTS tools increasingly viable for teams that are not able to meet in a single location.

VTS tools are useful in boosting involvement, strengthening team commitment, and improving the quality of the work that a team produces; all while reducing costs and minimizing wasted effort. Team leaders will continue to seek solutions that can log threaded discussions, manage structured and unstructured data, and provide scheduling and calendaring in a "just-in-time" fashion to meet team, executive, regulatory, and business-process management requirements.

Coordinating and keeping teamwork on track with smaller budgets is a profound challenge for any organization. The demands of a global marketplace continues to raise the bar for efficient operations, lower overhead, and optimization of resources, such as around-the-clock schedules for teams whose members are located across national boundaries and datelines. Regulatory compliance often requires full accountability with respect to dialog, documents, decision-making, and productivity. The tools necessary to manage teamwork, from general to specific, from social to multinational, from short-term to persistent (long-term), must have the right stuff to accomplish this job. The motivation to use the tools well and communicate effectively is the huge cost to the bottom line of miscommunication.

Now that we have introduced you to our holistic view of collaboration, the "people, process, and technology," I want to focus on some of the trends that have been emerging in both collaboration technologies and the collaboration market over the last few years. We provide this as background so that you can see the progression from where collaboration technologies and the market started and where they are going.

2 Trends in Collaboration

"Don't follow trends, start trends." —Frank Capra

The following 10 trends are pushing the evolution of Collaboration 1.0 to 2.0. Whether you are an IT manager, a venture capitalist, or a consumer, these trends will likely have an impact on your collaboration technology decisions. Each one is discussed in some detail, but, since many of these trends are all at an early stage of development, their full impact has yet to manifest:

1. Convergence of audio/video/data conferencing
2. Presence (and status) everywhere
3. Merging of synchronous & asynchronous collaboration
4. Enterprise collaboration convergence (and standardization)
5. Push to the infrastructure (for collaborative functions)
6. RTC market consolidation
7. Driving collaboration into industries and processes

8. Changing distribution channels

9. Changing buyers for collaboration solutions

10. Mobile collaboration (PDA/cell phone as platforms for collaboration)

Trend 1: The Convergence of Audio, Video, and Web (Data) Conferencing

In the 1990s, you could buy audio conferencing, or use an audio-conferencing bridge (a server with multiple ports to connect different phone lines into a conference call). You could also buy a room-based video-conferencing system. However, by the late 90s, Web- or data-conferencing systems were also available; not exclusively for larger corporations, but for individuals as well.

Vendors began to realize, however, that the stand-alone versions of these technologies had begun to fall short for end-user needs. Users were becoming more sophisticated in terms of their demands and less interested in having to tinker with applications to get them to do the things that they required.

Since then, vendors have been searching for a killer application that shows video and talking heads clearly without distracting delays, presents text, graphics, and image documents of any size, scales flawlessly and provides clear, crisp sound for live and pre-recorded voice, and other sound-based applications. Ideally, this would all be available on any platform, from a huge auditorium screen to a cell phone. Although it is not there yet, the trend is underway.

The initial push has included the following combinations of product features: Microsoft Live Meeting with Arel Anywhere (video conferencing), WebEx (now owned by Cisco) added voice and video, Oracle adds voice and video, Skype adds video, and so on.

There are also a variety of new video services that are worth mentioning. Viodia, for example, offers a service that lets you make high-quality video (MPG4) with a consumer video camera and then store, edit, and broadcast it via their service at a significantly lower cost than developing video with traditional technologies.

Altus has a service that does post-production on video and supports transcription and video indexing down to the word (most other vendors offer keyword search, or can index to a slide). This can be useful, for example, if you have a long training video and want to search for a specific reference in the audio portion of the video.

Unified Communications

One area where there has been great advancement is in the collaboration space called "Unified Communications" (UC) This means that the technologies for audio (PBX), video (both room-based and web cams) and Web/data conferencing, IM (instant messaging, chat), presence and location are all integrated into the communication infrastructure of the enterprise. There are many vendors focused on UC, including all the usual suspects: IBM/Lotus, Microsoft, Cisco, and the like.

The IBM/Lotus tool for IM, presence, status, and location is called "Sametime," and it integrates with IBM/Lotus Domino (Lotus Notes) on the asynchronous side. The latest iteration (Version 8) is due to be released about the same time that this book is published (Q1, 2008). IBM/Lotus is now offering three versions of Sametime, which also will integrate (through a new middleware layer) with a multi-vendor PBX and IP/PBX environment by Q2 of 2008. Figure 2 shows the three Sametime offerings.

In terms of delivery, Sametime "Standard" is available now, and is what IBM/Lotus has been selling as Sametime. Sametime "Entry" which is a light version mostly configured for integration with Microsoft Outlook should be available in Q1, 2008. The Sametime "Advanced" version which adds additional collaboration capabilities, should also be available in Q1, 2008. The Sametime integration with IP and standard PBXs will be in beta in Q1, 2008 and should be delivered to the market by Q2, 2008.

Lotus Sametime "Advanced"
- Persistent Chat
- Broadcast Suite (SkillTap, Instant Polls, Alerts)
- Instant Share
- Location Services
- Advanced Features via Gateway *(future)*

Lotus Sametime "Standard"
- Presence, IM, Web Conferencing
- Extensible Eclipse Client and SDK
- VOIP Chat, Video
- Location, File Transfer, Screen Capture
- Public IM Gateway Access
- Mobile Clients

Lotus Sametime "Entry"
- Secure IM, Presence
- Rich Text, Emoticons, Contact Info
- Contextual Collaboration

Lotus Sametime "Unified Telephony"
- Telephony Plug-ins for ST
- Click2Call, Click2Conference
- Aggregated IM, Phone, Calendar, Presence
- Incoming Call Control (Rules, Alerts)
- Connectivity to Telephone Systems
- Standards (SIP, CSTA)
- Legacy PBX/bridges

- *Release 2*
  - Voice Mail/UM Access

Figure 2: New Sametime Options and Unified Communications (UC) Integration with PBXs[3]

IBM also just announced the acquisition of WebDialogs, a web conferencing vendor that had about half a million users for their software-as-a-service (SaaS) offering. This acquisition helps IBM move the Lotus Sametime family of products more quickly into the hosted model and provides customers with choice and flexibility in how they buy and operate their web-conferencing services. IBM will also integrate the service with its collaboration portfolio, including IBM Lotus Notes and IBM Lotus Sametime software.

WebDialogs Unyte services will expand IBM's offerings in the web-conferencing space, particularly for the small-to-medium business (SMB) segment, as well as for departments within larger organizations. This acquisition moves IBM even further into the Unified Communications arena.

---

3. Based on an analyst pre-briefing for *VoiceCon* 8/15/07.

It is not that IBM has not been looking for one of the hundreds of RTC vendors to acquire. Before WebEx (the RTC market leader) was acquired by Cisco, they were in active discussions with IBM. However, when the CEO of WebEx called one of their partners (Cisco) and mentioned these discussions, Cisco bought WebEx on the spot for 10x earnings ($3.2 Billion).

Unified Messaging and Unified Communications

At the recent VoiceCon conference, which has traditionally focused on telephony infrastructures, a good number of vendors were talking about Unified Messaging (UM). Although the idea of UM—also referred to as Unified Communications (UC)—has been around for quite a while, it has recently gained some new momentum.

Although there is some disagreement in the industry as to what UM is, it generally refers to the result of combining various traditional communication technologies with newer ones. An example would be the integration of your corporate PBX for telephony (or your IP/PBX, if you have advanced that far) with the presence detection capabilities and information from IM/chat. This would all be integrated with e-mail, video and data conferencing, and mobile devices all with a common interface. Wikipedia defines Unified Messaging as, "the integration of different streams of communication (e.g., e-mail, SMS, Fax, voice, video, etc.) into a single or unified message store, accessible from a variety of different devices."

In his keynote address at VoiceCon, Gurdeep Singh Pall, corporate VP for the Unified Communications Group at Microsoft, talked about "communication enabled business processes." Microsoft had just released its Office Communication Server 2007. What was refreshing was that he was talking not just about *the technology*, but also about how it can be *applied* to business process. I was very happy to hear this. It showed that the industry is finally maturing—becoming aware of how technology must integrate with the people using it as well as with their critical and/or customary processes in a real way—a way that will make Collaboration 2.0 truly successful.

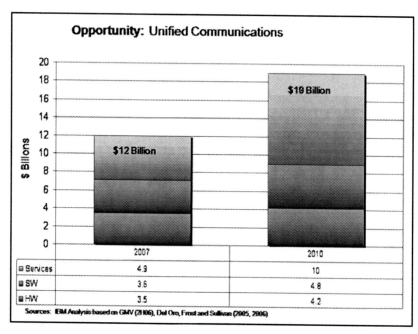

Opportunity: Unified Communications		
	2007	2010
■ Services	4.9	10
■ SW	3.6	4.8
■ HW	3.5	4.2

Sources: IBM Analysis based on GMV (2006), Del Oro, Frost and Sullivan (2005, 2006)

Figure 3: Showing the Opportunity in the UC Market

Figure 3 comes from IBM and shows the rapid growth it expects in the UC area, which explains the hot competition between Microsoft, IBM, and Cisco. Another smaller vendor, Avistar, which has a video conferencing background, is a leader in that technology for the financial services market, and is also going after the UC market (see Figure 4) in a more general way with their new software-only video offering.

Product: Integrated, Unified Enterprise Communication					
	Video	Audio	E-mail	Data	Chat
Collaboration	☑	☑	☑	☑	o
Presentation	☑	☑	☑	☑	o
Publishing	☑	☑	☑	☑	o

Figure 4: Avistar is Also Going After the UC Market

Sametime is a good example of a tool that is making presence, status and location information ubiquitous. Some of the competitors for IBM Sametime include Microsoft's Office Collaboration Suite and Cisco® Unified Communications system (a suite of voice, data, and video products and applications specifically designed to help organizations of all sizes to communicate more effectively). These vendors are being pushed by their customers into an integrated offering. This leads to Trend 2 about "presence," which seems to be the cornerstone feature that many of the vendors are building their integrated offerings around. From a people perspective these trends are positive.

The more varied and rich the communication channels the closer they approach the delivery of face to face communication.

Trend 2: Presence Everywhere

One of the most interesting aspects of real-time collaboration (RTC) technology is the ability to detect the presence of someone online. In addition, you can also tell their status, that is, if they are on the phone, typing on their computer, etc. Sometimes you can also tell their location: at their office desk, at their home office, out of the office (from the GPS in your cell phone), or in a conference room (from a smart badge).

Currently, the telephone on your desk cannot let you know if someone is available, online, on another call, or other specific status/state information for that person. The best you get is a hit-or-miss process that leads to a busy signal or voice mail.

Presence detection was initially tied to IM and "buddy lists" for chat rooms in the consumer market. However, like many of the Web 2.0 technologies, over the last few years these functions have evolved (particularly security) and have begun to appear in a new incarnation in the Enterprise. Presence also is appearing as a core capability in VTS and other collaboration applications.

Both Microsoft and IBM/Lotus have made big strides in this area. Microsoft now has server-side integration (federation) with Yahoo! Messenger (as of June 2006); Google offers the same integration with America Online (AOL) and ICQ (now part of AOL). Within Sametime, IBM includes federation with SIP/SIMPLE and XMPP communities, as well as AOL, Yahoo!, and GoogleTalk. Recently, Yahoo purchased Zimbra that uses Zimlets (Zimbra Widgets) to extend functionality. This should also make the presence issues more interesting at Yahoo.

Other vendors, such as Cisco (through WebEx) and Adobe, are looking to make presence detection available from within their entire suite of applications—one click and you get presence and status information about anyone currently included in your value network. For example, the cycle time for tasks can be greatly reduced if you can quickly locate, make contact, and reach decisions with key contributors (this is especially true for distributed project teams).

While this presence *stuff* sounds a little like "Big Brother," it can also be quite useful. Let's take a common work scenario that can cause quite a problem for current collaboration technologies:

A is working with B in a web conference on a specific document. They come to an impasse and need C to determine how to resolve a specific paragraph in the document. Today, either A or B has to go to their various buddy lists for each IM client (AIM, MSN, Yahoo,

Google Talk, etc.) to try to see if C is available. If that does not work, A must try calling C's office phone, cell phone, or pager to find them. Once A finds C, A can send her a link and bring her into the Web conference to resolve the impasse. However, there is no tool today that allows one to find C easily, wherever she may be. It takes about 12-15 clicks to bring C into the Web conference today, and is a very messy process for what should be a very simple collaborative interaction.

I asked David Marshak, Senior Product Manager for Unified Communications and Collaboration at IBM, if Sametime (even in its new configurations) would be able to support such a scenario. His answer was an unqualified "maybe."

Right now, Sametime does support a unified buddy list, so if C's presence were detected on that list, you could invite her into the Web conference (or an "Instant Share" session) with one click. However, if C was not on that buddy list, then A would first have to add C to the buddy list in order to find C in her community connected through the gateway or a *clearinghouse*. IBM, which already allows IMs (text chats, VoIP, and click-to-call) to internal users not on the buddy list, is working on a more ad-hoc method of reaching external contacts in federated communities, just by knowing their unique ID (e.g., e-mail address or mobile phone #). Some of the IBM gateways to PBXs will be operational (mid 2008) and should support this type of situation with greater ease.

I also proposed this scenario to John Coyle, Senior Director of Marketing at LiteScape. He too offered a solution through their product that allows the integration of a wide variety of presence information from such sources as: LDAP, Active Directory, buddy lists from Yahoo, AOL, etc., as well as Outlook personal contacts, IBM Sametime, Cisco CUCS, and mobile device presence protocols.

Trend 3: Integration of Synchronous and Asynchronous

There have been different rates of growth in the synchronous and asynchronous sides of the market. The asynchronous collaboration tools, including VTS, were developed and marketed first. They accounted for roughly all the revenue for collaboration from 1985 (when Notes was first developed and sold) through 1996 (when WebEx first came to market). Synchronous collaboration revenues rose rapidly from a $100 million in the mid-1990s to $0.5 billion in revenues by 2000.

Collaborative Strategies defines real-time—or synchronous collaboration (RTC) as audio, video, and data conferencing, including IM/presence-based applications and VoIP, as well as consulting professional services and hardware.

The year-over-year growth rate for synchronous collaboration technologies averages 14%. The asynchronous collaboration tools market had its big growth spurt in the late 1990s and is now growing more slowly, at an average of 12% between 2000 and 2008. Overall, the collaboration market is still healthy and growing at an average rate of 13% through 2008.

Combining Synchronous and Asynchronous

Over the past few years there have been indications, however, that asynchronous and synchronous technologies are coming together.

These indicators include:

- WebEx (synchronous) acquires Intranets.com (asynchronous)

- Microsoft Office 2007 adds elaborate synchronous/asynchronous collaboration functions

- Oracle Collaboration Suite (synchronous) adds Virtual Team Rooms (asynchronous)

- IBM/Lotus Sametime (synchronous) and Domino/Notes 8 (asynchronous) become intertwined

RTC growth rates have exceeded the asynchronous collaboration technologies growth rate almost every year except 2006, when they were equal, which we attribute to pent-up demand, along with a better understanding by vendors of how to effectively package and present these tools to the marketplace. The overall penetration rate of RTC technologies today is close to 30%, indicating a lot of room for growth, which we believe will continue throughout the rest of this decade.

Wikis

One of the areas in asynchronous collaboration that has grown rapidly over the last few years is wikis. CS has found wikis being used commonly in a number of places in the enterprise (usually in IT, R&D or Marketing), but the popularity of these easy to use tools is spreading; wikis are starting to pop up all over the place. ("Wiki" by the way, means "quick" in Hawaiian.) The most famous wiki is Wikipedia (which is not a good example for most wikis and what they do), but there are many other vendors of wikis and many open source (free) wikis in the market today.

Wikipedia describes a wiki as "a medium which can be edited by anyone with access to it, and provides an easy method for linking from one page to another. Wikis are typically collaborative websites, though there are now also single-user offline implementations. Ward Cunningham, developer of the first wiki, WikiWikiWeb, originally described it as "the simplest online database that could possibly work."

Wikis are great for collaborative projects. A wiki is perfect for this, because pages are so easy to edit and update, that everyone on the project can contribute. What is unique about wikis is that they drive (asynchronous) consensus through the wiki document. Because anyone (or all those you give access to the wiki) can add to the document and all of these additions and changes are tracked, and those that post to the wiki known, it engenders a discussion around what was posted and there is often consensus for the final version of a document. A good example of this is Wikipedia itself. Take a look at terms like "project management" and click on the "discussion" tab and you can see the discussion behind the published document.

Wikis, CMS, and the Enterprise

Some of the best-known wikis for the enterprise are SocialText and Atlassian's Confluence, both of which seem to be getting good traction. The most sophisticated enterprise wikis work with single sign-on security systems like Siteminder, or offer network and directory integration (LDAP and Active Directory) for user authentication and authorization.

A wiki is a collaborative website where users can create and edit pages. Wiki software has been around since 1995, but when wikis first came out there were not a lot of options for WYSIWYG editing from within a browser, so the wiki markup language (sometimes called "wikitext") provided a particularly valuable short hand for formatting text that was much easier to learn than pure HTML.

Wikis fall conceptually under the broad concept of content management, and you could certainly use your existing CMS (content management system) to create a wiki-like site. However, wikis are unique in that Wiki software empowers users to create and edit their own page. Content management systems provide tools for creating and editing content, too, and both offer a WYSIWYG interface that makes writing content for the web a lot like using a word processor.

These days, more wikis have WYSIWYG editing features as well, so the wiki markup language becomes a less interesting feature in terms of formatting, although it does provide the benefit of being supported by all browsers on all platforms, something that is typically not the case with rich-text editors. Many wikis support both wikitext and rich-text editors.

However, there is one area where wikitext still retains its power and where wiki software is different from a CMS: linking. Wiki software still provides a much easier way to link pages within the wiki to each other. Links are made based on the title of a page, so the author does not need to use, remember, or type long URLs in order to link one page to another. You can find a brief introduction to how this works in Wikipedia's entry for wikis.

Wikis emphasize ease of content creation. This simplicity comes mostly from many sources:

- A wiki markup language that provides a short-hand way of formatting text and linking documents.

- The ability of users to create and edit pages directly and independently.

- A bottom-up approach to site structure and navigation.

- Simple templates.

- A conscious decision to eschew workflow or even simple approval steps. (However, wiki tools like SocialText and Atlassian do support some workflows.)

Contrary to their reputation, wikis are content management systems that can be managed. They simply take a different approach to content management by choosing to emphasize speed and flexibility rather than strict controls. In order to successfully implement a wiki software package you will need to look at workflow from a different perspective and be sure to select wiki software that provides the right level of content monitoring and access control for your organization.

Many wikis today are offered as SaaS (software as a service), or even free as open source projects like: Twiki, Kwiki, Pmwiki, and MediaWiki.

Blogs and Discussion Boards

Industry analysts tracking the social software market predict it will grow from $226 million in 2007 to more than $707 million by 2010.[4] This represents an explosive compound annual growth rate (CAGR) of more than 41%! Much of this market is made of wikis, but some of these numbers are for social networks and online communities, both of which are also growing at a rapid rate.

---

4. SocialText Blog, Enterprise social software market data, http://www.socialtext.com/node/274, August 1, 2007

CS has seen some vendors that have used the same back-end and have added a front-end that the user can choose to be a wiki, a blog or threaded discussion (e.g., Q2Learning). What makes a wiki different from say a threaded discussion (forum or discussion board) or a blog?

Blogs seem to be single-threaded discussions that are more focused on publishing (with feedback) an individual's ideas or opinions. For a good example of a blog (and you are welcome to add some feedback) see the collaboration blog where many of the ideas in this book were expressed in their original form (http://www.collaborate.com). Some blogs like the popular TechCrunch have over 250,000 visitors a day. According to Bloglines there are about 6 million blog posts a day. Some people post multiple times a day, others once a day, and still others, like me, 2-3 times a week. Technorati shows about 1.6 million active blogs a day.

Threaded discussions, BBS, or discussion boards have been around for about 30 years, but got much more popular with the easy availability of the Internet. They are used for everything from distributed project team discussions in a secure project room, to open forums for feedback on a wide variety of vendor web sites. For a good example see The Motley Fool's discussion board on retirement investing.

Trend 4: Collaborative Consolidation in the Enterprise

Oracle may be a bellwether for convergence and standardization throughout the enterprise. Oracle—now a provider of an RTC suite—itself was using twelve different web conferencing systems before it decided to build and standardize on its own RTC tool.

Over the last decade, most large organizations have experimented with collaboration technologies, initially with asynchronous and then with synchronous technologies. All of the organizations had used RTC technologies (IM, webinars, or Web meetings) at least once at some point over the past year, and many were regular users of these technologies.

We noted that *different* groups within the organization were using *different* RTC technologies. For example, a training group might be using Saba's Centra or Adobe's (formerly Macromedia's) Breeze (now called Adobe Connect), while the sales group was using Linktivity's Inter-Tel, and the marketing group was using WebEx (now Cisco) or InterWise (now called AT&T Connect after the acquisition). This RTC proliferation has not gone unnoticed by IT departments, and, more and more, they have had to support users on all of these applications.

Due to this proliferation, IT departments began to consolidate on the basis of security, costs, politics, and existing relationships with certain vendors. This is not an optimal strategy for consolidation, not because of technical factors, but because of behavioral and social factors. With IT mandating a specific solution, IT may feel they have solved the problem more quickly, but in the long run it takes longer and costs more to get widespread adoption of the solution due to lack of "buy-in."

An alternative strategy would be to identify and interview all of the stakeholders using the different collaborative applications. Find out how they use the features to accomplish what tasks and how satisfied they are with their solution. Then, armed with this information, have an IT or a third party (like CS) develop a plan for consolidation. From that plan, a cycle of feedback and adjustments could result in an application that meets best meets user needs. It's not unusual for this consolidation process to take two years in a large enterprise, and even with stakeholder input, the process is very political.

Ironically, in many cases, the outcome of both strategies is the same. Microsoft, Oracle, Cisco or IBM/Lotus may still be selected as the corporate collaboration vendor, and their RTC tools used. It is for this reason that the market leader in RTC, WebEx was in a tenuous position, one from which they were able to remove much of the risk by merging with Cisco. This was a smart move for both WebEx and Cisco, as it brought Cisco's infrastructure expertise together with WebEx's desktop and Web application expertise.

Trend 5: Pushing Collaboration into the Infrastructure

Since collaboration is a behavior, one day all software will support it, and like the ever-present plumbing systems in your house, collaboration technologies will be part of the computing infrastructure. Although in its early stages, CS already sees movement in this direction.

Figure 5 shows the different functional categories that comprised the collaboration market as well as the direction in which these functions are starting to consolidate. That is, all of these independent functions, over the last few years have been blending into the central square (Distributed Project Management, Virtual Workplace and Process tools).

In this functional area, we find a variety of tools that have aspects of customer relationship management (CRM), document management, knowledge management, innovation management, virtual team systems, portals, online communities, social networks, discussion threads and forums, and even some RTC functions.

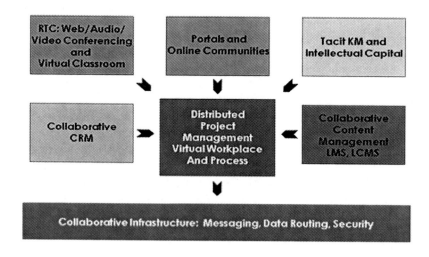

Figure 5: Convergence of Collaborative Functions and Movement into the Infrastructure

As the continued value and effectiveness of this integration stage is established, the next phase is that these collaborative functions will essentially become transparent as they move (primarily with Microsoft at the helm) into the system infrastructure layer that currently deals with e-mail, security, directory structures, and so forth. Windows Vista is a good example of this in that it has more collaborative functions in it than Windows XP. Certain versions of Vista (Ultimate, Pro) even include Groove Networks functionality (a collaborative application which Microsoft acquired when it bought Groove from Lotus a couple of years ago) in the operating system.

Trend 6: Market Consolidation

From 2003 through 2006, a number of acquisitions resulted from the fact that large software vendors see collaboration as a critical function that they must either develop or acquire. Microsoft acquired Groove Networks, WebEx acquired Intranets.com for $45 million—and was in turn itself acquired by Cisco for $3.2 billion; eBay acquired Skype for about $4 billion in cash and stock. With Microsoft's acquisition of Groove, it was clear that the 800-pound gorilla was moving into the collaboration market, and now had a way to start to go after the small and medium business (SMB) market—which represents approximately 10 million potential customers. Microsoft now offers a number of online (SaaS) applications under the Microsoft OfficeLive brand.

WebEx's acquisition of Intranets.com appears to have been a response to the Microsoft acquisition of Groove because Intranets.com focuses on the SMB market and also adds asynchronous functionality to the WebEx product mix, resulting in WebEx WebOffice.

Other significant steps toward consolidation over the past several years have included the following events:

- eBay buys Skype (VoIP), PayPal, and invests in Craigslist

- Yahoo buys eGroups and Zimbra

- Oracle buys PeopleSoft and Siebel Systems

- BEA (which may be bought by Oracle) buys Plumtree

- Google buys Deja, Outride, Pyra, Applied Semantics, Kaltix, Sprinks, Ignite Logic, Neotonic, Picassa, JotSpot, Writley and Keyhole

- Documentum acquires eRoom, and is then acquired by EMC

- IBM recently acquired WebDialogs after losing WebEx to Cisco, they also acquired FileNet and Watchfire

The collaboration market is still very fragmented, with a few large players, and hundreds of smaller players. Over the next few years, there will most likely be six to eight large vendors with horizontal collaboration offerings; many of the other players will have to move into niche markets around specific horizontal processes or vertical industries.

Trend 7: Driving Collaboration into Verticals and Critical Processes

Market consolidation means that many of the vendors currently in the market will be gone or absorbed within the next two or three years. The larger players, such as Microsoft, IBM/Lotus, Cisco/WebEx, and a few others, will own the horizontal play in the collaboration space. This means that the hundreds of other collaboration vendors in this space will either have to adapt their applications to ride on top of what Microsoft, IBM or Cisco offer as platforms, or find a specific vertical niche that they will be able to defend, or move out of the market altogether.

A good example of this is OpenText. A few years ago it had several collaborative applications (FirstClass, LiveLink, etc.), but it decided to focus on their core competencies (Enterprise document and content management, governance and regulatory compliance) and let Microsoft deal with the collaboration issues. Over the following year, OpenText moved their applications on top of Microsoft's products to form its collaboration platform (Exchange, Communicator, etc.), effectively moving OpenText *out* of the collaboration market. Others have focused on specific niches like the SMB market, financial services, or collaborative data analysis for oil and gas exploration.

Critical Processes and Collaborative Leverage

It is important to look at processes that are critical to the business (i.e., the business would fail without them), and find the processes that have "collaborative leverage." Collaborative leverage occurs when collaborative technologies are applied to critical processes in the right way to realize big benefits (maybe a 30%-40% decrease in cycle time). By contrast, when collaborative tools are applied to the wrong processes (usually transactional), then there is little collaborative leverage, and not a noticeable productivity increase.

Below is a list of critical business processes that have collaborative leverage and some specific examples for each process where collaboration technologies can be applied.

1. Sales & Marketing (proposal development)

2. Customer Service/Support (exception handling)

3. R&D (new product development)

4. Value Network Management (relationships with external organizations, DPM, and project management) (exception handling)

5. Training (internal and external)

6. Decision support/crisis management

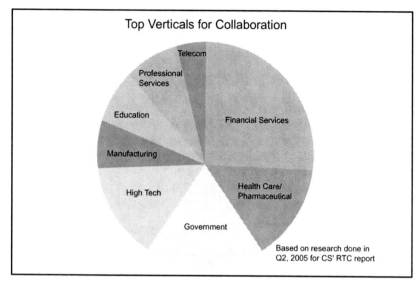

Figure 6: Industries Adopting Collaboration Technologies Most Readily

Figure 6 shows the results of our primary research on which vertical or industry markets are adopting collaboration technologies most readily. The people buying collaboration solutions today are no longer just IT people, but more and more they are line-of-business managers and consumers (or "prosumers," as some like to call them) More on the new buyers of collaboration technologies in Trend 9.

With more collaboration functions available today as SaaS applications—often offering a free "try before you buy" option— much of the risk involved in adopting, investing and working with these applications is greatly reduced.

Trend 8: Changing Distribution Channels for Collaboration

The collaboration market is about 30 years old and over the last 10 years (with the introduction of the Internet as a platform for collaboration) has started to mature more rapidly. Because of this, the channels that have traditionally distributed collaborative applications and services are changing. Mergers are creating new opportunities for moguls in one industry to become serious providers of products and services in another. For example, Google is moving from its position as simply king of search engines to czar of communications and business networks (more on this later).

In 2003, many vendors offered RTC functionality as a service only. Since then, most vendors have had the wisdom to understand that they should not let the distribution methodology get in the way of the sale. To that end, most RTC vendors have their offering as both a service and a product. Even WebEx, which was purely service-oriented, now allows customers to purchase a site license for their software. Today some analysts estimate that about half of all collaborative applications are hosted offerings (SaaS).

Also between 2003 and 2005, telecom and VoIP sales through the channel have increased with some 18%. In 2003, only 25% of revenues went through the channel (based on CS primary research), but by 2005, 43% of revenues were going through the channel.[5] This rapid increase signals a major shift to commodity status for these services over a short period-of-time. The same trend is true from 2005–2007, and the rapid commoditization of VoIP as well as other collaboration services such as: IM/Chat, Web/data, audio and video conferencing, wikis, blogs, online discussions, as well as document and content management systems.

In looking at the adoption life cycle for the channel for collaboration technologies, CS found that the channel often lags behind that of vendors by two to three years. What this means is that a new technology introduced and available directly from the vendor usually appeals to the early adopters or innovators. Once the technology has been

---

5. Collaborative Strategies, *2006 RTC Report*, http://reports.collaborate.com

used and reviewed in the field, the integrator/VAR channel will begin to make these technologies available to the more cautious early majority and late majority buyers. Since many of the early adopters and innovators were buyers of collaboration technologies in the late 1990's during the "tech boom" period. In 2000, the tech bust rapidly followed the boom, and for a period of about three years, there was not much buying going on. However, in 2003 the market for collaboration technologies began to pick up, and by 2007 it has become one of the hottest markets in high tech.

The only catch is that there is no market for collaboration, but rather for collaborative applications or solutions that are put into the context of specific business needs, processes, and problems.

Ma Google?

Telephone companies typically own some sort of network and offer telephone service and access to high-speed Internet connections. Now, so does Google. So should people start calling the search giant a phone company? Not yet, but some Google Inc. watchers say it appears to be headed in that direction. Speculation about Google's phone company aspirations is not new, and has been rekindled with recent moves by Google. It has been insinuated that they may commit $4.6 billion or more to buying the wireless spectrum in an upcoming auction.

Speculation is that if Google does acquire the wireless spectrum (which is being made available as U.H.F. stations convert to digital signals), it will likely push an open-platform approach and act as a wholesaler allowing other companies to resell a variety of services. Add this to Google's recent investment in UbiquiSys, a British start-up that makes base stations intended to boost wireless coverage inside homes and buildings, and you can start to discern a strategy for Google's focus on the wireless business.

In early November, Google unveiled "Android" a new mobile phone software platform. Thirty-four companies have said they will join the Open Handset Alliance, a multinational alliance that will work on developing applications on the Android platform. Members of the alliance include mobile handset makers HTC and Motorola, U.S. operator T-Mobile, and chipmaker Qualcomm.

The Android platform consists of an operating system, middleware, a user-friendly interface, and applications. Consumers should expect the first phones based on Android to be available in the second half of 2008.

Open Source

What Kazaa did to change the music-buying dynamic (providing peer-to-peer availability of songs at a manageable price), a number of innovative companies are beginning to do with VTS.

The proliferation of Open Source applications and their rapidly growing acceptance in the business world, as well as the move toward the Web browser as the great equalizer platform, means that changes to operating system control of the desktop will become much less relevant in the next few years. As we have seen with collaboration technologies, particularly VTS, software services are being hosted online, providing users with the most up-to-date code versions, quick fixes, and access from anywhere.

As with other technology areas, there is a growing trend in the development of fully Web-resident, Open Exchange technologies to place VTS in the open source environment. IBM recently put some of its software into the open source arena. The software part of the equation is straight forward: a combination of open-source, standards-based (ODF) office applications, and Lotus Notes/Domino messaging software. Overall, the software package offers applications for e-mail, instant messaging, Web browsing, social networking technologies and ODF-based productivity software (including word processing, spreadsheets and presentations) that can run in multiple PC environments.

Specifically, software includes IBM Productivity tools that support the OASIS Open Document Format (ODF), the Firefox Web browser, Lotus Notes & Lotus Domino, Lotus Sametime and IBM WebSphere Portal v6 on Red Hat Desktop Linux suite, or Novell SUSE Desktop Linux.

But IBM is not the only collaboration vendor to venture into the open source arena. Akiva now offers Silk, an open source collaboration platform that "competes functionally" with Microsoft's SharePoint and IBM's WorkPlace. Silk is available under the terms of the GNU General Public License (GPL) or under a more restrictive commercial license that provides additional company support. Zimbra, which is also based on open source, is taking on the big guys by positioning its product directly against Microsoft Exchange.

Other Open Source VTS tools include: Phpgroupware (which includes 50 different applications), and CollabNet that are customized for distributed software development groups. Even Novell has released a collaboration tool into the Open Source arena—a collaboration server called Hula). Oracle is rumored to be working with Mozilla. Oracle's main motivation in working with Mozilla on the Lightning project is likely the desire to create a competitor to Microsoft Outlook and is now owned by Yahoo!

In a recent eWeek interview, Ward Cunningham, creator of the wiki, suggested that the power of collaborative development has only just begun to be realized and that Open Source software will continue to spur more collaboration and more innovation. Cunningham, who was formerly with Microsoft and is now the director of community development at the Eclipse Foundation, said "Open Source software will continue to grow and thrive because it enables user innovation." [6]

One of the advantages of Open Source applications is that the people building them are not part of an IT data fortress, but rather have greater exposure to the Web 2.0 revolution occurring in the consumer space. In addition, the style of working in open source (swarm) is more like a very distributed project team that is using online collaboration tools to help move the project forward.

6. Darryl Taft, Father of Wiki Speaks Out On Community and Collaborative Development, *eWeek*, March 20, 2006

Trend 9: Changing Buyers for Collaboration

Geoffrey Moore, in his book *Crossing the Chasm: Marketing and Selling High Tech Products to Mainstream Customers,*[7] identified a standard cycle in which organizations acquired technology.

In the 1990s, vendors could sell collaboration technologies to both innovators and early adopters (to the left side of the chasm). Some of the characteristics of these populations were:

- They were interested in the technology itself

- They had the budget for new technologies

- They had the vision to know where to apply the technologies

- They had enough clout to try the technology on one or more groups

- They were looking for the technology to provide a competitive advantage

Today most collaboration vendors are selling to the "Early Majority" (to the right of the chasm) and this population has a very different take on technology:

They tend to be:

- Risk averse; they want to know it has worked for others in their organization or field.

- Technology neutral (at best); and looking for the technology to be largely transparent to process.

- Looking for a solution to a specific set of problems that fits with their current infrastructure, requires little or no training, and as an intuitive ROI.

---

7. Geoffrey A. Moore, *Crossing the Chasm: Marketing and Selling High Tech Products to Mainstream Customers,* (New York: Harper Business Essentials, 1998)

Buyers today are purchasing fewer horizontal collaboration technologies (e-mail, IM, VoIP) and are more interested in solutions to their specific problems that just happen to include collaborative functionality (Zimbra, WebOffice, etc.).

Along with competitive differentiation, this is another reason that many vendors in the collaboration space are moving into vertical and process-specific markets

- Blue Marble to Demonstrate Enterprise Collaboration Tools in Geographic Calculator v7.0 at GITA for Oil & Gas Solution Spotlight

- Open Text and The Frontline Group to Partner on Oil and Gas Industry Software Solutions Tailored to Improve Collaboration in Exploration and Production

Not only can they continue to charge a higher margin (because the perceived value is higher), but those market niches have not yet been commoditized—that is, become part of a clearly recognized need—to encourage significant competitive solutions. Developing a niche solution requires highly specialized knowledge and expertise about the vertical market or industry and its processes to make sure the solution fits. Ideally, the vendor can boast a major industry brand as a reference customer, and has applied their product to a problem very similar to that of the prospect.

Vendors who run a demo for this type of (early majority) prospect will likely get a "Wow!" though they may not get more. The problem here is one of translation; where the Early Adopter and the Innovator both enjoy the technology itself, are willing to look for a problem just to get a chance to apply the technology, and have the vision of how to apply it once they find it. Early Majority group members do not have the interest in the technology for its own sake—they have a plenty of real problems they must solve and are only interested in technologies that promise do that.

Often, a potential buyer/user of collaborative technology does not actually know what they need and are less willing to take a risk in buying and implementing an inappropriate solution. They prefer to take a wait-and-see approach, believing they cannot afford to make a purchasing mistake, and letting others prove efficacy first.

Case Study for Buying Collaboration Technologies: AEC

When asked what problems kept him up at night, the sales director of a large company in the Architecture, Engineering, and Construction (AEC) industry, answered, "Losing proposals to the competition." More investigation revealed that his team's access to the people and materials it needed were preventing them from responding to RFPs on time. So even though his organization was growing and was putting out more proposals than when they were smaller, it wasn't putting them out fast enough to keep up with the competitive changes in the market. He was losing sales to competitors, to the tune of $60M per year (based on losing one sale averaging $5M each month).

Ironically, when it was pointed out that his problem was a collaboration problem, he did not see it and as a result saw no value in a seeking a collaboration technology solution. What he was willing to buy was software for proposal development. He chose a package that just so happened to incorporate collaborative functionality, and, inadvertently allowed his team to access the materials and expertise they needed to tap into more quickly. His sales improved dramatically but for reasons other than what he anticipated.

Self Service

One of the trends gaining momentum is that of "self service". As organizations become flatter and leaner, the Web is taking up the slack in providing access to information, extending sales opportunities, and building better customer and value-chain relationships. Customers themselves are more sophisticated now, demanding access to readily available information early and often: to support a purchase decision or solve a problem after they've bought a product or service. They are more likely to place orders online, download products (software or other intellectual property products), upgrade an existing product, or service, use Web-based free or subscription applications or services, or contact other users who can provide first-hand experience on using a particular product of interest.

As companies are downsized, the individual employees within the company are actually *upsized*. That is, more value is placed on the knowledge and personal network of affiliations each individual employee can draw upon as a resource. Additionally, with the role between employee and customer beginning to blur, as are the boundaries between what's considered "inside" and "outside" the company, the workflow—and hence the associated technologies—must flex to accommodate the new working environment.

This flexibility is reflecting in applications being developed as SaaS. A great number of collaboration software tools are now being offered in the SaaS, model, according to industry analysts, by 2008 half of all software tools will be offered as a SaaS. The worldwide SaaS market reached $6.3 billion in 2006 and is forecasted to grow to $19.3 billion by year-end 2011.

Often technology users don't have control over the development of the solutions they need to solve their daily work challenges. It seems increasingly less efficient to explain their problem to IT and have to continually tweak what they get in return, before it works the way they want it to. They would rather take the proverbial bull by the horns, spend a few hours cobbling together an application (out of pre-existing modules, if available), customize it for their particular need, and feel like a hero when they can roll it out to their group quickly and in working order. They don't want to wait for a lengthy IT evaluation, nor do they want to be dependent on some overworked (sometimes territorial) IT person to respond to their requests for changes.

One well-established VTS vendor, SiteScape, recognized the self-service trend several years ago, and has been developing and responded with a clever strategy. They created a number of portlets (also called gadgets or widgets)—or reusable Web components—that display relevant information to portal users, such as their e-mail, the weather, the status of discussion forums, and news reports based on topics of identified interest and so forth and can be cobbled together easily. SiteScape actually developed a portlet economy, by allowing third-party developers to create and market integratable portlets. When a portlet is used, the developer of the portlet and SiteScape share the sale. Other vendors have mimicked this same approach, including: Zimbra with Zimlets and Google with its Gadgets.

This type of business model motivates innovation and collaborative development, and it ensures that the entire developer network gains valuable information about user needs and is able to meet them quickly. Sharing the wealth in this way, takes some of the development burden—especially for highly specialized portlets—off of wiki-like SiteScape and increases their ability to fine tune offerings to meet the needs of their customer. This high level of user participation in the development of applications and content is another trend we have seen in the Web 2.0 evolution.

Other collaboration vendors that are embracing this self-service trend include:

- Salesforce.com's AppExchange

- Skire (drag and drop forms tool for project management)

- Open-Xchange

- eProject (Summer Edition)

- WuFoo (online HTML forms builder and database)

- Qwaq (3-D rooms for interaction)

- OpenSAM – an Office-like integration framework

Mashups are another fast-growing approach to addressing the self-service trend. The term "mashup" was first coined by the music industry where DJs would mash up bits of songs together to create new, live, hybrid compositions. Technology enthusiasts adopted the term, which is now used to describe the phenomenon of crafting hybridized applications built from data or functionality found across a number of different, smaller applications connected together through a common application program interface (API). This is a huge area—especially in the Web 2.0 Open Source community—and one we will discuss in greater depth in our online community (http://collaborate.com/book).

Trend 10: Mobile Collaboration

Mobile end-points are becoming more capable; they are smarter, have more storage, and allow you to have a window into your desktop information from anywhere. With more cell phones in the world than PCs (even laptops), it is no wonder that software vendors have seen this platform become a higher priority as an end-point and a way for mobile information workers to collaborate with their colleagues and team members. As the components continue to shrink and wireless network technologies become more sophisticated and less expensive, these handhelds will expand on the capabilities we already see now in the market place: voice, pictures, video/broadcast, e-mail, and full Internet access.

According to S. Keslev in his April 2005 article in the ACM SIGCOMM *Computer Communication Review*, cell phones are already a growing platform for Internet access. However, currently, a low percentage of cell phone users access data through their devices. A recent Pew Internet and American Life study found that only "10% rely on mobile devices for voice, texting, or entertainment."[8]

That number will undoubtedly jump dramatically in the next two to five years, due to both technical and non-technical factors and the obvious advantages of a highly mobile platform. These factors include low cost, ease of maintenance, well-established providers, manageable form factor, over-the-air upgrades, power management, and other characteristics that favor this platform for growth. The implications for teamwork are clear. If workers can take lightweight devices with them anywhere; access materials and discussions on a team space; communicate with audio, video, text, and data transmissions; they will be even freer and more apt to work from wherever they are, whenever they can.

ZD Nets IT Facts Blog indicated that by the end of 2003, there were 1.4 billion cell phones serving about 25% of the world's population. In comparison, there were only 607 million PCs (including both desktops and laptops), and a negligibly small number of PDAs. Cell phones continue to maintain this lead because of a rapid rise in subscriber numbers in

---

8. S. Keslev, Why Cell Phones Will Dominate the Internet, ACM SIG-COMM. *Computer Communication Review*, pg. 83.

China, India, and Russia. In 2004, China reported 310 million users, about 25% of its total population, and India saw an increase of 11 million, or 25%, and reached a total of 44.5 million subscribers. In Russia, mobile phone subscriptions jumped 65% from 36.5 million in 2003 to 60 million by September 2004.

According to one industry analyst group, the number of smart phones doubled between 2005 and 2006 to 98 million, while the number of cell phones worldwide continued to rise to an estimated 1.85 billion. Tomi Ahonen and Alan Moore, researchers in the cell phone industry and authors of the book "Communities Dominate Brands," discuss how digital technology is rapidly changing the way people are doing business. These authors estimate that there were 2 billion cell phone users in 2006. That means that every third person on the planet is a cell phone user.

Advances in PDA/Smartphone screen real estate have had a significant effect on the adoption of the cell phone or smart phone platform for serious collaboration. In 2007, the U.S. is still woefully behind in wireless infrastructures. Currently: EDGE, 3G, UMTS, EDvO, WiFi, WiMAX, etc. were all implemented quickly in Asia and a bit slower in Europe. The U.S., on the other hand, has yet to implement these cellular and broadband infrastructures, and this has left us woefully behind.

It is common in Japan or Korea to have the bandwidth to do cell-to-cell streaming video using 3G technologies like Universal Mobile Telecommunications System (UMTS). This is even possible in some places in Europe, but nowhere in North America. We have become a third-world country around an infrastructure that we invented.

Cell Phone Real Estate

The limited real estate offered by the PDA/cell phone screen has presented a challenge compared with that of a full-sized laptop. One option is to make the displays for mobile devices larger, but that is counterproductive to making these devices smaller and more portable. Faster, more efficient displays in new sizes and shapes are continually announced at shows like CTIA.

Today's mobile operating systems have begun to support dynamic switching between portrait and landscape viewing modes to help accommodate content and layout more effectively. There are several Pocket PC (Windows Mobile OS) devices with increased resolution (VGA 480x640 and QVGA 240 x 320). HTC has recently released a new device called the Advantage X7501, running the Windows Mobile 6 OS, and has a 5-inch VGA screen and a magnetically locking detachable keyboard/cover (see Figure 7).

Figure 7: The HTC Advantage X7501, More PDA than Phone

Expect to see multi-window (although very small) video conferencing applications on PDAs and true mobile collaboration by 2008 (in the U.S.). Already some web conferencing is available on cell phones, in fact, WebEx (now Cisco) is rumored to have one brewing. Other web-conferencing vendors, such as Persony, for example, can do video conferencing using Flash 7 mobile (though I was unable to successfully install it on my Windows 5 mobile device at this printing).

My Phone/PDA

I have an iMate Jasjar, which is made by HTC in Taiwan and called the Universal, is a 3G phone. It cannot really operate in full glory on the 2G infrastructure here in the U.S. While it could do mobile video conferencing—provided it had a 3G UMTS network—it can't. The phone actually has two cameras, one on the front side of the phone for conferencing and another (1.3 megapixel) on the back of the phone to take photos. The QVGA (320 x240) screen and full QWERTY keyboard makes the iMate Jasjar, in my opinion, a better PDA (especially with a 4GB SD card in it) than a phone.

Figure 8: iMate Jasjar, the HTC Universal: A Re-branded 3G Phone

Communication is Still Key

However useful the interpersonal communications, there seems to be something missing from the 10 trends that have just been mentioned. The trends relate to the channel or pipe, the machinery that moves the communication between two or more points. What's not included in the trends, which is essential to effective communication, is what's in the content of the messages delivered, and how to make these messages impactful, useful, and truly in service of collaboration. Some suggestions:

- Tutorials for how to communicate in ways that enhance collaboration as an industry standard

- Templates that help drive dialogue a certain way such as: crafting "Agreements for Results" or through the "Cycle of Resolution"

- Programs that catch certain words

3 The Evolution of Electronic Collaboration

"The theory of evolution by cumulative natural selection is the only theory we know of that is, in principle, capable of explaining the existence of organized complexity."—Richard Dawkins

The Virtual Herd

Why do people communicate, collaborate, and form social networks? Nigel Nicholson in an article in the July/August 1998 issue of *Harvard Business Review* believes that people have an innate need to communicate and build community; that it is hard wired into the human brain. Notes Nicholson, "You can take the person out of the Stone Age, but you can't take the Stone Age out of the person."

When *homo sapiens* emerged some 200,000 years ago, survival required group living much as animals live in herds. The "herd" is an important Stone Age concept because it introduces the notion of dependency. "I am loyal to the herd because it protects me from danger; it feeds me and shelters me. This dependency is a relationship I want to preserve, so much so that it actually becomes a need, and, in the Stone Age, a survival trait."

When we talk about animals, we talk about herds; when we talk about people, we talk about communities or societies. On an evolutionary scale, the human herding instinct has hardly changed at all, says Nicholson, even as our environment has evolved, though not always at the same pace in different parts of the globe. This leads to new challenges in communication and community building.

A "herd" could be thought of as a single node in a network. Nomadic tribes consisted of several herds that met and separated during the course of their travels, passing news about sources of food and water, trading posts, dangers and other useful information to help each other out. Having a network of herds strengthened the tribe. A herd that stops moving is a community; communities as they grow become countries and civilizations and devise newer means to communicate across time and distance.

In today's disaggregated communities, people with mutual interests "come together" virtually though they may be separated by distance, time zones, race, religion, socio-economic status, politics, gender or other segregating factors. The same requirement for interdependence prevails: "I know what I need, but I personally don't know who can fulfill that need for me, so I need to expand my personal network, by finding someone who knows someone (who knows someone who knows someone) who can help me."

Hence, the notion of community (or herd) is still as valid as it was in the Stone Age; however the modern day implementation has undergone a transformation. The new community is a "virtual herd." I see social networks as extensions of our "personal networks." In the past your personal networks were limited by geography, today that is not so. Let's look at Facebook as an example: "...about 85% of students in supported colleges have a profile up on Facebook. That's 3.85 million members, with 60% log in daily, about 85% log in at least once a week, and 93% log in at least once a month." [9]

---

9. TechCrunch, http://tinyurl.com/2g7q7r, September 7, 2005.

Blogs, personal and organizational websites, social networking sites, mutual benefit exchange and e-commerce sites, as well as the burgeoning mobile-phone-based solutions, are all examples of new-age means that serve a fundamental drive—born of human instinct—to build community. The rapid proliferation of user-generated content (YouTube) is a testament to the importance of this phenomenon, and our innate instinct to be part of the herd. This is evidenced in social behaviors (unconscious or not) to overcome barriers of geographic and social distance to form community.

Technologies for Interaction

A number of technologies today have evolved to help support this human need for connectivity. Posting a document on the web so that someone else can read it does not constitute collaboration; there must be some level of interaction for collaboration to occur. If that person reads your document and responds to you via the web, no matter the length of time between the posting and the response, then THAT is an interaction and constitutes web-based collaboration.

Figure 9 shows this evolution graphically. It shows first human interaction with data and content (1970's and 1980's), then shows asynchronous interactions through BBS postings (threaded discussions) and web sites in the mid-late 1990's, and finally the ability for people to interact with each other directly (and synchronously) around content, which has only occurred in the last decade. The best example of this is a web/data conference.

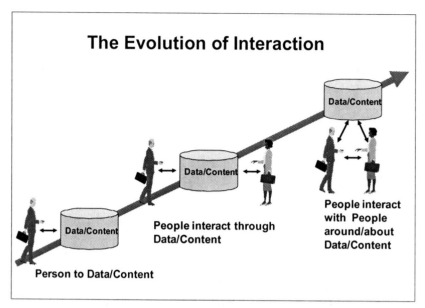

Figure 9: The Evolution of Interaction

Collaboration technologies evolved from earlier communication techniques and they began to incorporate "coordination," (working on tasks together over time for a specified goal). Table 1 looks at how communication technologies have grown more complex over the last century, yet more and more of the administration of these technologies has moved from experts (like telephone operators) to the user.

Collaboration is more than just the coordination of tasks over time; it also involves innovation and the sharing of information and knowledge. It involves trust.

	Telegraph	Telephone	Fax	E-mail	Virtual Team & Workplace Software	Web-based VTS tools
	1800s	1900s	1970s	1980s	1995-2015	2005+
	1-to-1 Communication	1-to-1, party lines, conference calls	1-to-1, 1-to-many (broadcast fax)	1-to-1, 1-to-many (broadcast e-mail)	Many-to-many communication for virtual teams.	Many-to-many communication for virtual teams.
	Standardized & secure service for written communication over distance for coordination.	Immediate delivery of audio communication across large distances instantly.	Phone and scanning technology for faster delivery of written communication over distance	Fastest delivery of written communication & digital files across large distances in hours or minutes.	Shared access to a secure master document. Interactions measured in hours or minutes.	Shared anytime access to secure documents, management
	Specific end poring, poor security, can't broadcast, limited alphanumeric messaging.	No visual element or ability to included documents. Fax becomes adjunct functionality.	Sequential info flow; editing, & changes difficult to track / share; each copy degraded; color not available.	De-Facto standard for team communication. Sequential process does not support team work well.	Enables group communication & coordination but may not target critical processes.	Structured asynchronous communications: Threaded discussions, shared calendars.

Table 1: Evolution of Communication to Collaboration Technologies

Chapter 3: The Evolution of Electronic Collaboration

A 30,000 Foot View of Collaboration Technologies: First-, Second-, and Third-Order Effects

Disintermediation is effectively the breakdown of existing channels to an end. A discussion in Wikipedia (which itself disintermediated paper-based encyclopedias like Encyclopedia Britannica) notes that the term was originally used in the banking industry in about 1967 in reference to consumers investing directly in securities rather than leaving their money in savings accounts. This term was later applied to borrowers going directly to capital markets rather than to banks.

The Internet, because it lowers the cost of communication to virtually zero, has helped to make a variety of processes more efficient. Driven by economic forces, these efficiencies have had a strong impact in disintermediating several industries.

Amazon.com initially disintermediated book stores, and later, retailers in general. Now, Amazon is offering a wide variety of hosting services called Elastic Compute Cloud (EC2) virtual hosting service. They also offer Amazon Simple Storage Service (Amazon S3), which enables storage in the cloud. These services are now so complete, inexpensive, and available, that they are starting to spawn a plethora of new businesses that use Amazon services for their complete infrastructure (a new product called Openfount makes use of the Google Web Toolkit and Amazon S3). Openfount's big idea is that a solo developer ought to be able to deploy an AJAX application to the web without worrying about how to scale it out if it becomes popular. If you park the application's HTML, JavaScript, and static data files on Amazon's S3 storage service, you can make all that stuff robustly available at a cost that competes favorably with conventional hosting). Other applications appearing on Amazon Services include: Geezeo, Webmail, and SmugMug (online photo storage and sharing). Altexa targets small businesses (for backup), while ElephantDrive and JungleDisk target consumers.

In a recent press release from Persony, Eric Chen, the CEO, stated "Persony has created a solution that uses open-source web and video servers, such as Apache and Red5, which can be hosted on Amazon Web Services at a cost of 1 penny per participant hour or $1 per hour for 100 participants. In comparison, a hosted Adobe Connect Professional meeting costs $0.32 per participant minute or $1,920 for one hour with 100 participants."

iTunes did the same type of disintermediation for music stores and record companies; Netflix pulled the same trick on Blockbuster and other video retailers. Craigslist has largely disintermediated classified ads in most newspapers.

In our assessment, collaboration technologies have also had a significant disinter-mediating influence. This influence, if looked at over time, can be divided into three phases, which can be referred to as first-, second-, and third-order effects.

First-, Second-, and Third-Order Effects

Tom Malone, a professor at MIT Sloan School, produced an article in August of 1991 with John Rockart entitled, "Computers, Networks and the Corporation."

This article discusses the effects that information technologies are likely to have on corporate structure and management approaches. By dramatically reducing the costs of coordination and increasing speed and quality, these new technologies, according to Malone and Rockart, will enable people to coordinate more effectively, to do much more coordination, and to form new, coordination-intensive business structures. It is from this article that we draw our orientation to the first-, second-, and third-order effects of *collaboration* technology.

Malone and Rockart explain:

> *To understand what is likely to happen as information technology improves and its costs decline, consider an analogy with a different technology: transportation.*

> *A first-order effect of transportation technology was simply the substitution of new transportation technologies for the old. People began to ride in trains and automobiles rather than on horses and in horse-drawn carriages. As transportation technology continued to improve, people did not use it just to substitute for the transportation they had been using all along.*

Instead, a second-order effect emerged: people began to travel more. They commuted farther to work each day, were more likely to attend distant business meetings, and began to visit far-away friends and relatives.

Then, as people used more and more transportation, a third-order effect eventually occurred: the emergence of new, "transportation-intensive" social and economic structures. These structures, such as suburbs and shopping malls, would not have been possible without the wide availability of cheap and convenient transportation.

What Caused the First Internet Bubble?

Dr. Malone saw this pattern in technology adoption (and its effects) some 15 years ago. Using the same model, we have been able to see how collaboration technology evolved in the following areas with these associated effects:

1. **Publishing** (content)

2. **Connection** (social media)

3. **Community** (permanent online social structures)

Content is King

In the first-order effect, people took ads, brochures, articles, and most anything they had written, and put it up on the web. Between 1995 and 2000, that is mostly what we saw, with an emphasis on the creation of web sites and portals for the aggregation and display of content. The big technologies that came out of this were search (Google) and portals like Yahoo! and MSN.

This effect caused the first Internet bubble around the turn of the century/millennium and was a virtual gold rush. The metrics of measurement at that time were "eyeballs," which unfortunately did not translate into revenue, and so, in 2000, the bubble burst.

However, the disintermediation of traditional methods of information or content distribution is still going on. Travel and real estate agencies, newspapers, radio, and TV, along with channels in many other industries are facing disintermediation with formerly hidden content now becoming transparent to the consumer or business.

Connection—The Second-Order Effect

Around the most recent turn of the century, the second-order effect was emerging and setting us up for the second Internet bubble, in which we find ourselves floating now. What people discovered was that the Internet was great not only for sharing content (the focus of the first-order effect) but also for connection, especially to discuss that content with other people. This gave rise to discussion forums, online dating, IM chat, blogs, social networks, wikis, cell-phone texting (SMS), and many other technologies and products all focused on helping people connect with others online. This effect is not as mature, but it can already be seen through sites like Jeteye, Flickr, and YouTube, where people can post, share and comment on all types of content.

YouTube was purchased last year by Google for $1.65 billion, Flickr was acquired by Yahoo, and NewsCorp bought MySpace for over a half billion dollars. Currently Facebook, another social network, has refused buyout offers in the billions, but did recently take an investment from Microsoft of $425 million, which values Facebook at about $15 billion.

In the spring of 2007, Facebook opened up its API so that other developers could take advantage of the Facebook social network. To date, about 5000 applications have been built upon Facebook, and has increased its value many fold. Several venture capital firms (like Bay Partners) are now funding start-ups that are putting applications on the Facebook platform.

Today, we live in a smaller, and somewhat more prudent, bubble with increasing VC investment in companies that help people connect around content on the Internet. However, the investors in the first bubble learned a hard lesson and they are not willing to take such great risks. So today, rather than just presenting "slide-ware" and expecting to get funded, you must have actually built the product or service and have it up and running—ideally, with paying customers or subscribers (better still if the customers have some brand recognition) and already producing revenue. Today venture capital investment (after many VCs got burned in the first bubble) is about limiting risk.

The biggest risk is that the product/service never gets developed; the second biggest risk is bringing it to market; and the third biggest risk is that customers or subscribers will not like it or be willing to pay for it. Since it costs so much less today to build an application (you can host it on Amazon services), other Venture funds like the Charles River Quick Start program offer small amounts of capital to get good ideas started. Joe Kraus, founder of recently acquired JotSpot, wrote a now famous post in Business 2.0 called "Retooling the Entrepreneur" in which he talked about the difference between launching Excite.com ($3,000,000) and Jot ($100k). In that post, Joe said

"The sources of funding capable of writing $100,000 checks are a lot more plentiful than those capable of writing $3,000,000 checks. It's a great time to be an angel investor because there are real possibilities of substantial company progress on so little money."

Virtual Social Structures—The Third-Order Effect

Because many of Collaborative Strategies clients are vendors of collaboration technologies, they have been directly affected by this second-order effect, and many of them have asked, "What's next?" The typical response is: If content was first, and people connecting and talking about content was second, then people interacting with people (yes, content is still important) will likely follow. As a social scientist—with a technical background—I know that when people start to interact, especially on an ongoing basis, they immediately start forming social structures.

These third-order effects of collaborative technologies make it easy for people to form and support virtual social structures (aka communities and social networks). The third-order effect is just starting to happen, and it will cause a third and even more prudent economic bubble towards the end of this decade as these technologies start to gain popularity.

There are an enormous number of online social network and community tools available now, including:

Q2Learning, iCohere, Affinity Circles, GroupMembersOnly, Google Groups, Yahoo Groups, SocialText, Collanos, Foldera, Near-Time, Leverage Software, Smallworldlabs, Social Platform, Web Crossing, CollectiveX, Me.com, Sparta Social Networks… and the list goes on.

The types of tools offered by these applications include many functions we have already discussed:

- User Profiles
- Visual Targeted Matchmaking
- Expertise Discovery
- Community chat
- Integrated opinion polls
- Private messaging (IM)
- Blogs
- Wikis
- Quick connect
- Multimedia file sharing
- Customized notifications
- Tagging, tag clouds, and social tagging
- Presence
- RSS feeds
- Discussion forums
- Group and role administration
- Integrated calendar management
- Rating and ranking of content
- Reputation engines
- Sponsorship and advertising engines
- Community e-mail marketing
- Community activity reporting

They support a number of different types of communities:

- Customer communities
- Media communities
- Internal/enterprise communities
- Consumer communities
- Partner or channel communities
- Event communities
- Member communities
- Project communities

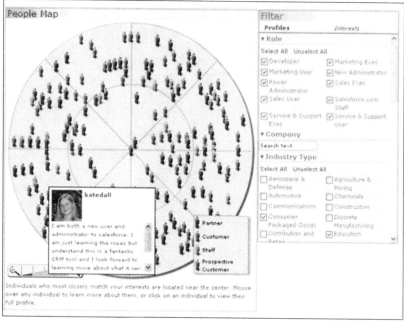

Figure 10: PeopleMap from Leverage Software (Social Networking)

Many of these are Web 2.0 companies that embrace the principles of transparency, ease-of-use, agile programming, little or no training required, and speed to market.

Chapter 3: The Evolution of Electronic Collaboration

Responding to Second- and Third-Order Effects

The Collaboration Technologies Conference has even decided to rename itself to Enterprise 2.0, which acknowledges the shift in the role collaboration technologies plays on the Internet through Web 2.0 technologies and also the effect these technologies are having on different organizations.

Many online community providers are trying to crack the code and take advantage of this third-order effect. Yet none has gotten the right mix of features, ease-of-use, and compelling content to become a dominant player, although it does look like Facebook with their now open API is the lead player in this arena.

However, there are other online communities that don't have hundreds of millions of users, but are hard to ignore. Second Life has over 10M users (more on Second Life in the next chapter), World of Warcraft (part of the Massive Multiplayer Online Gaming [MMOG] industry) has over 8 million players (Figure 11 shows over 6.5 million in 2006[10]), and Lineage has over 14 million players. This industry segment should be worth almost $10 billion by 2009.

---

10. From http://www.mmogchart.com.

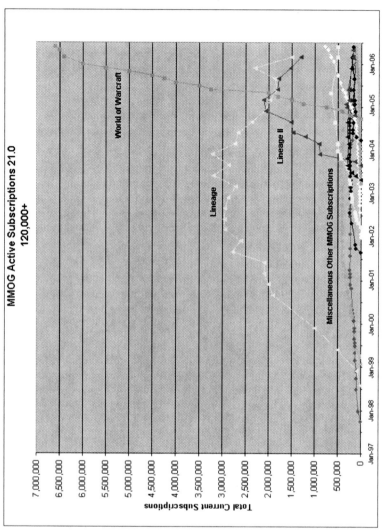

Figure 11: MMOG Subscriptions

     Chapter 3: The Evolution of Electronic Collaboration

Driving Revenue from Communities in the Third Bubble

It is most likely that someone will find a way to monetize communities the way Google got "ad words" to monetize search to drive revenues in the second bubble.

Right now, most of the players in this space are smaller, more innovative companies, many of which are start-ups. These companies have a small window of opportunity to make their mark and either become major players or be bought up by one of the larger software vendors (which we expect to happen in the 2007-2008 timeframe).

Many of the larger players in the collaboration space (Microsoft, Cisco, Citrix, IBM, Adobe, etc.) will begin to see this third-order effect as an opportunity. Increasingly, companies are beginning to recognize online communities as an important way to collaborate with their customers, support transparency, and drive revenues through ongoing interaction.

These larger companies are starting to shift their product focus to support online communities—other than those related specifically to their technology—over the next year or two.

But what do these effects mean to the end user? In the consumer space, expect to see more collaboration applications appearing as Web 2.0 services (SaaS). Also expect to see collaborative functionality broken down to the level of a widget or gadget. A snippet of code you can put on your web site will allow you to talk with people that are on your web page, or detect the presence of colleagues when they look at a document and notify you on your cell phone that they have done so.

With the increasing number of mashups both inside and outside the enterprise, expect to see some real changes in the areas that IT controls. IT will still maintain control over the traditional ERP applications, but will probably give up control of "opportunistic applications" to the end user or line of business (LOB), who will do mashups of their own to create these small applications that IT will never get to. With hundreds or thousands of these opportunistic applications happening in an enterprise, the ROI does eventually look good. However, the challenge for IT is access to the data that end-users want to mashup to. How is it possible to keep the data integrity high and the data secure in these dynamic environments? The other issue that does not seem to be as critical in the consumer space is accountability.

If you do a mashup within the enterprise and the resulting data is wrong or bad in some way, and others use it, and the company ends up losing money or worse, then who is responsible or accountable for the mashup? The people that did it are not professionals and will probably point to IT. IT did nothing with the mashup and probably did not even know about it. The best thing that IT can probably do is to provide guidelines and best practices that will help to cut down on the number of mistakes made from mashups. By providing these guidelines, they can determine if the end-user doing the mashup actually followed the guidelines, and if not, IT has some deniability, and the end-user is in trouble.

Since these are very new areas for the enterprise, it will probably take a while to figure out what the best practices and guidelines for Enterprise 2.0 world are. Most likely by the end of the decade standard policies in corporations to deal with opportunistic applications will have become commonplace.

Perhaps even more important than the technology best practices and protocols will be the communication and interaction standards. We have seen some of this in terms of eBay users, but we have the potential to create communities with the kind of communication standards many people long for.

4 Collaboration 1.0

"Collaboration on a book is the ultimate unnatural act."—Tom Clancy

Collaboration 1.0 was mastering the art of working with others who were essentially co-located. They were in close physical proximity, so you could touch, feel, see, and even smell them as you worked together. That made collaboration easier, but as Thomas Friedman pointed out in his book of the same name, *The World Is Flat!* and that has demanded new kinds of tools, processes, and awareness.

Focus on Content

From 1990-2000, most collaboration was focused inside the enterprise or around groups and teams within an organization. Figure 12 looks at the evolution of the Web from 1.0 – 4.0, right now we are in Web 2.0 (the social web), but by the end of the decade (given the pace of technology innovation) we should start to move into Web 3.0 (the semantic Web) regardless of naysayers.

We can see some of this starting through the standardization of APIs that have helped the thousands of mashups to occur. A *mashup* (web application hybrid), according to Wikipedia, is "a web application that combines data and/or functionality from more than one source."

We also are starting to see bots, intelligent agents and "augmented meeting environments" beginning to emerge as part of Web 3.0 (but more on those later).

This figure starts in the lower left and shows some of the tools and characteristics of Web 1.0, which I like to call "the content web."

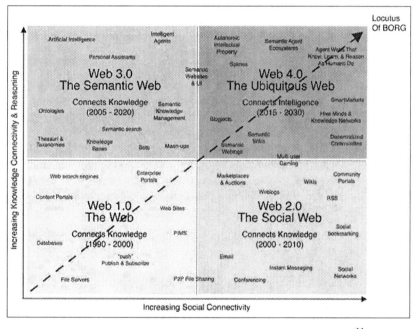

Figure 12: Evolution from Web 1.0 to Web 4.0[11]

Web 2.0 came to describe almost any site, service, or technology that promotes sharing and collaboration right down to the Net's grass roots. That includes blogs and wikis, tags and RSS feeds, del.icio.us (social

11. From Nova Spivak, Radar Networks & Mills Davis, Project 10x.

tagging) and Flickr, MySpace, and YouTube. Because the concept blankets so many disparate ideas, some have questioned how meaningful—and how useful—it really is, but there is little doubt it owns a spot in our collective consciousness. Whether or not it makes sense, we now break the history of the Web into two distinct stages: Today we have Web 2.0, and prior to that, there was Web 1.0, which was mostly the "content and search" web. With Web 1.0, we published static web sites, which people could read but there was little interaction. With Web 2.0, web sites are much more dynamic and there is a recognized interaction between people.

Interestingly, a recent Pew study found in a survey that 73% of U.S. adults own a cell phone, 68% have a desktop computer, 30% possess a laptop, and 73% connect to the Internet, but very few use them to express themselves publicly via Web 2.0 applications. The study defines Web 2.0 users as people who take advantage of technology "to express themselves online and participate in the commons of cyberspace," including maintaining a personal Web site, blogging, vlogging, remixing media or sharing new-media creations. *Only 8 percent of U.S. adults are "deep users" of Web 2.0 features.*[12]

Web 2.0 vs. Enterprise 2.0

The Web 2.0 *movement* has been gathering strength over the last few years. It espouses not only technology philosophies (ease-of-use, web-based, true multimedia, the use of broadband and mobile technologies), but also suggested behaviors (transparency, immediacy, participation, responsiveness, etc.). But Web 2.0 is very different from Enterprise 2.0: where Web 2.0 is a consumer phenomenon, Enterprise 2.0 is more focused on how to apply these technologies in a more secure and managed way to a well-known population.

Some of the characteristics that define Enterprise 2.0 include:

- Choice of distribution, SaaS, or licensed software
- Can be bought as a series of services

---

12. Candace Lombardi, *Wired But Not Web 2.0? That's Normal Study Says*, http://tinyurl.com/2hhub8, May 7, 2007.

- Maintenance and support are separate services and don't always have to be purchased from the vendor but can be acquired from an ecosystem of partners (SAP offers third party maintenance through its TomorrowNow unit to Oracle apps customers)

- Bug fixes and upgrades happen automatically for all customers (on a service)

- Tools to provide process management, configuration, conversion, integration, testing, systems management, and end user training minimize expensive labor

- All service partners are vetted and certified

- Support transparency on product/service quality, customer support, etc. (as service)

- Provides a clear API and certification for integration of third party software (e.g., salesforce.com's AppExchange, Facebook API)

- Actively encourages an on-line developer/integrator community and pushes for an "open source" licensing of community intellectual property

- Is transparent with the customer about components/services, discounts and taxes

- Shares progress with customer base (part of transparency) on a regular basis on implementation and support metrics (salesforce.com provides metrics on its on-line performance)

What are some of the characteristics of Enterprise 1.0? What is driving the Enterprise to change to 2.0 (the characteristics and drivers are summarized in Table 2).

**Table 2:   A Comparison of Enterprise 1.0 and 2.0
Characteristics and Drivers**

Enterprise 1.0	Enterprise 2.0	Drivers
Static content and web pages, focus on content	Dynamic content, focus on interaction	Consumer Web 2.0 and social networking tools
Messages pushed by e-Mail	Information pulled through RSS feeds	Users want to personalize their information.
Content produced, and edited according to policy	Content from blogs, wikis, and other participatory sites	User created content
Asynchronous interactions (e-mail)	Synchronous interactions (IM, Chat and SMS)	Net Generation, growing up with computers
IT imposed control of technology	Individuals use new technologies and create content	Situational applications, and IT backlog
Search and Browse for information	Publish and subscribe to information feeds	Overwhelming amount of information available
Transactional oriented interactions	Relationship oriented interactions	Expertise discovery, cross organizational teams
Organizational Taxonomy	Folksonomy	Tagging of content for individual use
One application for everyone	Individual and niche applications	IT backlog and situational applications

Tools like wikis are taking hold in the enterprise, especially in the R&D, IT, and Marketing areas. The use of online communities for customer service and support is also getting traction. But things move a bit more slowly in the enterprise than in the consumer space, and I expect it will take the rest of the decade for these Web 2.0 technologies to morph into something that does not scare the pants off of an IT person, and to get widespread adoption across the enterprise. However, the biggest push back from IT folks is in regard to security.

Collaboration and Security

Since September 11th, 2001, security is at the top of many people's minds, terrorism is a constant news topic, and the majority has learned to adapt to the security measures at the airports. The directives have grown out of the Homeland Security Act for all government intelligence agencies to be willing and able to share information easily with each other. They must collaborate. But with increased access to information comes the accompanying increase in security risks.

From my experience consulting with several of the three-letter-acronym agencies, I can tell you that the cultures there are anything but collaborative, and between the "turf wars" and a culture of secrecy, it is hard to imagine even mandated collaboration being successful.

Security and collaboration do not have to be in conflict. Rather you can develop an infrastructure that can support both behaviors. Traditionally, the most frequently used tool for collaboration is e-mail. There are an estimated 30 billion e-mails sent every day (of which 20 billion are likely spam). When you consider that e-mail is not secure, that is a lot of opportunity for security breaches to occur.

Oops!

I recently received an e-mail from the CEO of a well-known software company. In it, he asked for a review and comments on the company's sales forecasts for last year. I realized right away that the message and the attached files had been sent by mistake and were really meant for another "David;" he'd simply selected the wrong e-mail address from his list and now I was looking at confidential company information and could have perused the finance spreadsheets as well if I'd wanted to. I was, of course, discrete. And when he later called, realizing what he'd done and asking me to ignore the message, I promised I would. But the situation was embarrassing for him and a security blunder of the first order.

Despite the lack of security, billions of private communications are sent around the globe with a touch of a button every day. One of the things we need to balance in collaborating with others is risk against reward. Our communication gets to the other person faster than snail mail, so the cycle time for many (collaborative) processes is quicker. This is a big benefit, and cycle times can be reduced even further with instant messaging IM/Chat) and other real-time collaboration tools.

No Substitute for You

Thus far, no collaboration technology takes the place of F2F meetings. However, they can go far to *augment* such meetings. Initial meetings are best in person, to establish trust with the other person (or people) before each is willing to share information (and collaborate). Humans pick up 75% to 80% of situational information about another person from visual, olfactory, auditory, gestures and other such physical cues. Once a relationship has been established, then it is much easier to continue on electronically, with e-mail, IM, or other collaborative technologies. If you simply can't be there in person, online collaboration is the next best thing.

There seems to be a generational issue around this, for example, for Baby Boomers (1943-1963) and older adults, the initial F2F meeting seems to be required because that is how we learned to establish trust. However, that does not seem to be the case for the "Net Generation" (1977-1997), who grew up with computers and meeting others online (and trusting them), seems as natural to them as breathing.

Today's distributed teams probably are a mix of generations, which can pose a problem for the team manager, as he/she might have to support different styles for different team members.

Security and Collaborative Selection: A Case Study

In 2005, we consulted with a Silicon Valley tech company that was interested in standardizing on IM and Web-conferencing tools across its organization (Stage 4 in our Evolution of Collaboration in the Enterprise model – see Chapter 15). We did our usual assessment and set off to interview all of the stakeholder groups. What was interesting was that the customer support group—which was on the East Coast—was one of the biggest users of IM (for back channel chat while on the phone with a caller), but was the least worried about IM security.

When we asked about this, they replied (a bit defensively) "This is not secret stuff we are talking about, and even though IM is not encrypted and is going out in plain text over the Internet, how is someone going to find a specific IM in all the billions of IMs that are happening every minute?"

When we talked with other groups within this organization, they all seemed to have a different view on security, and the company also recently hired their first "security officer". Fortunately, our assignment was not to develop a security policy for the enterprise. We talked with the new security officer, who was horrified by what he saw, and was working furiously to develop a security policy for IM and web conferencing for the organization that would likely be patterned after their intact e-mail security policy.

In working with other clients in more regulated industries (e.g., Financial Services, Health Care, Government, etc.), security and governance issues were much more top-of-mind, and often were a deciding factor in selecting a collaborative technology for the organization.

But no evolution occurs in a vacuum. Even while we were using Web 1.0 technologies, early adopters were starting to use Web 2.0 technologies. So now that Web 2.0 is in full swing with consumers and starting with the enterprise, what does this foretell for Web 3.0?

Web 3.0: The Semantic Web

Web 3.0 or the "Semantic Web," as it was named by Tim Berners-Lee, who invented the (first) World Wide Web. In essence, "the Semantic Web will be a "place"—a combination of technologies, systems, networks, standards, workflows, taxonomies, ontologies existing in the ether of cyberspace—where machines will be able to read Web pages much as humans read them. It will be a place where search engines and software agents can better crawl the Net assembling bodies of context-sensitive content based on explicit and implicit requests. While Web 3.0 will not be any more interactive then Web 2.0, per se, it will feature a greater degree of standardization for coupling content, applications and meaning, along with better tools to find people, web objects and content."[13]

---

13. Tim Berners-Lee, Semantic Web Road map. http://tinyurl.com/gtbxb, September 1998.

The Semantic Web isn't a new idea. This notion of an interdependent network of machines that can better read, understand, and process all that data floating through cyberspace first entered the public consciousness in 2001, when a story appeared in Scientific American. Coauthored by Berners-Lee, the article describes a world in which software "agents" perform Web-based tasks we often struggle to complete on our own.

In the chapter on Collaboration 2.0, we will discuss how these trends are coming together with trends in collaboration to make a whole new online experience, one which may just improve upon F2F meetings or other in-person interactions. These new augmented interactions will be called Collaboration 3.0.

The Semantic Web will have bots and intelligent agents that can do many things: check potential appointment times against others' schedules, keep track of new entries across the web that meet a user's interest profile, automatically book your next vacation, or research your term paper. If intelligent enough and you invest them with enough of your personal power, such agents might even be able to attend meetings for you, for the first time in history allowing you to be two places at once.

How will this actually work? In Berners-Lee's view, it involves a reannotation of the Web, adding all sorts of machine-readable metadata to the human-readable Web pages we use today.

Six years after the Scientific American article, official standards describing this metadata are starting to move into place—including the Recourse Description Framework (RDF) and the Web Ontology Language (OWL)—and they're already trickling into real-world sites, services, and other tools. Semantic Web metadata underpins Yahoo!'s new food site. Spivack's Radar Networks is building a kind of Semantic Web portal. A development platform called Jena, is in the works at HP, and Semantic Web structures exist already in Oracle's Spatial database tool.

Annotating the whole Web could be a daunting process, so other strategies are being employed. One early example is a browser plug-in called BlueOrganizer from AdaptiveBlue. In certain situations, when you visit a Web page, this browser plug-in can understand what the page is about and automatically retrieve related information from other sites and services. If you visit a movie blog, for instance, and read about a particular film, it immediately links to sites where you can buy or rent that film.

Another option available by having smarter agents is to put more tags (metadata) into the web pages, which would make the content, rather than the agent, smarter. Whatever the strategy, we are a number of years away from the Semantic Web, but at the rapid rate at which Web technologies progress, we may be using agents to do intelligent searches or booking appointments in the not too distant future.

5 Collaboration 2.0

"One Man's Transparency is another's humiliation."—Gerry Adams

Collaboration 2.0 has many of the same characteristics of Web 2.0 including:

- Ease of use

- AJAX (Asynchronous JavaScript and XML), a web development technique used for creating interactive web applications. The intent is to make web pages feel more responsive by exchanging small amounts of data with the server behind the scenes, so that the entire web page does not have to be reloaded each time the user requests a change. This is intended to increase the web page's interactivity, speed, functionality, and usability, front end or user interface

- Transparency (honesty or ability to see more about you or your organization as in a profile, etc.)

- Interactivity and participation

- The ability to create mashups of data or functions from several sources

However, Collaboration 2.0 can be more than that.

Collaboration 2.0 includes all of the outcomes, benefits, and values of Collaboration 1.0 but can take place in a virtual world, or in cyberspace via the computer. It requires an evolutionary leap in relationship building with others in a global, networked, cross border, cross industry, cross department, cross-functional environment.

Necessity is the mother of invention. As we moved to a knowledge-based economy with multi-national organizations, it became an imperative to work closely with others we may never meet face to face. That fact of organizational life has driven us to the new frontiers of Collaboration 2.0. The challenge many have taken up is that of: *developing the same capacity, creativity, and competence to work efficiently and effectively with our virtual colleagues across the boundaries of time, space, culture and the same complex challenges inherent in working with other human beings in the ever-changing external and internal landscape.*

Jessica Lipnak and Jeffrey Stamps of NetAge, who wrote the forward to this book, describe this as the "virtual gap" or how a virtual team replaces the lost context they would get in a F2F interaction. I believe this "gap" problem is mostly seen by Baby Boomers and not the Net Generation, in that the Baby Boomers still use e-mail as their main means of communication, while most Net Geners don't use e-mail but use IM or SMS as their main communications conduits.

9X Better Than E-mail

E-mail technologies are 30 or more years old. So if they are such ancient technologies (in Internet time), why does everyone use them? John Gourville, in Harvard Business School's Marketing department, did research investigating why so many new consumer products fail to catch on with their intended audiences despite the clear advantages they offer over what's currently on the market. He talks about the '9X problem' or the "...mismatch of 9 to 1 between what innovators think consumers want and what consumers actually want."[14] The 9X

---

14. J. T. Gourville, "Why consumers don't buy: The psychology of new product adoption." (Harvard Business School Note #504-056, 2004).

problem goes a long way toward explaining the tech-industry folk wisdom that says: "To spread like wildfire, a new product has to offer a tenfold improvement over what's currently out there."[15]

Andrew McAffee, Harvard professor and Web 2.0 guru, who was the keynote speaker at the Enterprise 2.0 Conference in June 2007, noted that "E-mail is virtually everyone's current endowment of collaboration software. Gourville's research suggests that the average person will underweigh the prospective benefits of a replacement technology for it by about a factor of three, and overweigh by the same factor everything they are being asked to give up by not using e-mail. This is the 9X problem developers of new collaboration technologies will have to overcome."

Collaboration's Wicked Problems

"Half our life is spent trying to find something to do with the time we have rushed through life trying to save." – Mark Twain

Time is a human construct, yet for many of us it can be one we accept as a cruel taskmaster. In collaboration, time is critical, but so is quality; tasks, events, and meetings are scheduled and must be coordinated among the participants to support collaboration and what comes out of that coordination. Yet, how many times has it taken 12 different e-mails to set up a simple meeting or conference call with three to four people. It is the *death of a thousand cuts* and the type of wicked problem that has Collaboration 2.0 vendors working "overtime".

Another problem is meeting quality and outcomes. There are no VP's of Meeting Quality at any of the companies with whom we have consulted, and yet at the majority of companies most people complain about "bad" meetings. Technologies are beginning to address this problem. YON Software's MeetingSense, for example, helps to address the ongoing problem of meeting quality by linking to most any web conferencing software (IBM is a reseller, and it integrates with Lotus Notes) or using it in an F2F meeting (without web conferencing). MeetingSense capture consoles not only helps to structure the meeting

---

15. Andy Grove, "Churning Things Up," *Fortune*, July 21, 2003.

for a better outcome, but it also captures information and outcomes (decisions or tasks) that result from the meeting and helps to make sure they don't just disappear into the void, as is most often the case.

Although MeetingSense does not deal with meeting process, or have specific templates for best practices (like for a budget meeting, or a project update meeting), one of the founders of MeetingSense, Hannon Brett, has stated that they are thinking along these lines.

TimeDance to TimeBridge

Meeting scheduling, is, at best an inefficient process. TimeBridge is the evolution of an idea that started about 5-6 years ago with a start-up called TimeDance. Unfortunately, TimeDance was a victim of the dot bomb era, but one of the founders is now advising the TimeBridge team.

Today, to schedule a meeting, the process most likely contains the following arduous steps:

1. Check your time

2. Send broadcast e-mail

3. Hold times on calendar

4. Collect and interpret responses

5. Negotiate a time

6. Rebroadcast to update participants

7. Collect and interpret responses

8. Confirm time

9. Remind and re-confirm

10. Pray…you don't have to re-schedule

How It Works

The goal of TimeBridge is to make the process of negotiating a meeting time more efficient. It integrates with your Google or Outlook calendar via a downloadable toolbar plug-in and works with internal and external participants' calendars even if they are not using Outlook. You can easily propose multiple times for a meeting, collect responses from all involved parties, and act on them.

TimeBridge cuts meeting scheduling down to five steps:

1. Pick a time/date for the meeting and invite attendees.

2. Attendees respond.

3. The meeting is confirmed and conflicts are resolved.

4. Share information with attendees (online meeting space for agenda and documents).

5. The meeting takes place.

The application provides a central place from which to review all of the meetings you have set up, look at meeting details, take any actions needed to resolve conflicts, and make other changes to the information (names, meeting locations, agendas, etc.) as required. Figure 13 shows the Invitation screen in TimeBridge reached by clicking the "New Meeting" button on the Outlook toolbar. You enter the e-mail addresses of those individuals you would like to attend, which come from your Outlook contact list or other sources.

Figure 13: Setting Up a New Meeting in TimeBridge

Figure 14 shows the next step: Looking at your calendar to determine your free/busy times. You can select up to five possible meeting times (in orange) and propose them to the meeting attendees.

TimeBridge is not a calendar, you can't store an event on TimeBridge, but because it integrates with Microsoft Outlook or Google Calendar it allows you to see events stored in those calendaring systems.

The biggest problem initially in using TimeBridge was when no one responded to an invitation. In the new version of TimeBridge, in cases where meetings cannot be confirmed due to availability conflicts, TimeBridge provides a wizard-like tool that suggests up to three different actions you can take to resolve the situation.

Time Brokering is a way to offer meetings at the same time to multiple people. As an industry analyst, this can come up all the time, for example, at a trade show where all the PR people want time for briefings. What the user can do is look at the show schedule and select some times over the two days they will be at the event and give all of those times (through TimeBridge) to the PR people that request time. That way the user does not have to do hundreds (literally) of e-mails about scheduling, and can let TimeBridge do it, on a first-come-first-served basis.

Figure 14: Looking for Free/Busy Times in TimeBridge

The Cost of Time

TimeBridge is initially a free service focused on "prosumers"—individuals who are professionals and might not be in a large organization that runs Microsoft Exchange servers, and yet need to schedule on average eight meetings a week. If Collaborative Strategies is an example of a "prosumer," then TimeBridge should do very well, and possibly even spread virally as their marketing plan suggests.

In this day and age of multi-tasking, meetings over a meal are a common occurrence and integrating with services like Open Table (restaurant reservations) or concierge services should be high on anyone's list of partnerships. CS sees a number of large partnerships for them in the near future, as well as the connection to other services that will enhance the user experience. However, they are also just the type of company that Google loves to snap up (like Writley and JotSpot). It will be interesting to see what TimeBridge looks like a year from now.

Some New Options

Volutio also has a new tool that goes by the name of ikordo (formerly codenamed Meeting Agent). ikordo does not require a download and communicates with invitees via e-mail. An organizer visits the ikordo site to plan a meeting, and doesn't require the invitees to change their current process in any way (which seemed to be some of the problem with TimeBridge). Invitees send e-mail responses allowing ikordo to build an availability calendar. Once replies are received, ikordo will find a time suitable for all invitees and schedule the meeting.

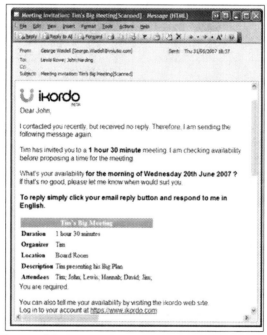

Figure 15: Negotiating a Meeting in ikordo

This communication method provides the flexibility to respond from any e-mail-capable device, even a Blackberry, remote access, or web mail—useful when a user is away from their primary workstation. Furthermore, ikordo takes the viewpoint that an invitee may not have an updated calendar or want to restrict or reserve portions of their availability. Ikordo will allow an invitee to share as many or as few of the details as desired with an organizer. This also gives the invitee the ability to share different availabilities with different organizers. For example, an invitee may give a wide range of availability to meet with their CEO, but a minimal number of times to meet with an outside salesperson."

Volutio has recently released a plug in for Microsoft Outlook that allows you to schedule a meeting using ikordo directly from a tab in Outlook. In Figure 16, you can see the new form they have created for initiating a meeting. This Outlook form allows you to add attendees based on your Outlook contacts. Your Outlook calendar also gives ikordo a starting place to schedule a meeting based on your availability. ikordo will keep the same functionality in acting like your virtual assistant and asking users about their availability and negotiating with your attendees until a meeting time is agreed upon.

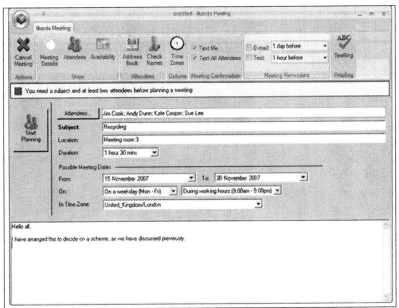

Figure 16: Creating and Scheduling a New Meeting from the Outlook Plug-in

Tungle in the Jungle

Tungle is a meeting coordinator that was launched into beta in March of 2007. Tungle has a plug-in that integrates with Outlook, Lotus Notes, and Google Calendar. The plug-in allows users to add people to their 'buddy' list and share calendar information. Inviting attendees to join a meeting provides a shared calendar of their availability and allows the organizer to pick a meeting time or let the software find the next available time slot (Tungle Wizard).

Tungle's biggest strengths may be their use of P2P (peer-to-peer) communications, so that no shared availability is placed on a server—an asset to security. Tungle uses a proprietary P2P protocol for the messaging transport. An additional strength of Tungle is that it allows users to maintain their current calendar provided it is one of the three mentioned.

In a recent briefing, Marc Gringas, the CEO of Tungle, noted that Web calendaring has not relieved the problem of integrating and sharing desktop calendars. The figures below show that Web calendars are only a small fraction of desktop calendar use, and, that if Google calendar is gaining ground, it is doing so at the expense of other Web calendars, not desktop calendars.

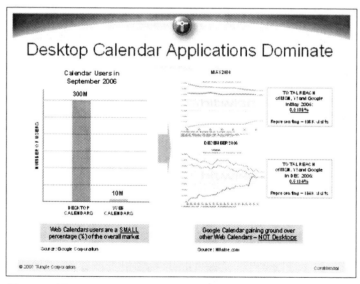

Figure 17: Tungle Research on Desktop Calendaring

Although we are seeing many Web 2.0 applications, there does not seem to be a slowdown in the use of desktop e-mail clients (mostly Microsoft Outlook) and calendaring. Industry analysts predict overall growth to be fairly rapid through 2010, which means that your desktop PIM (Personal Information Manager) is not going to go away, as a matter of fact, many desktop PIM's even sync with PDA's so that meetings or appointments can even be tracked when one is not at their desk.

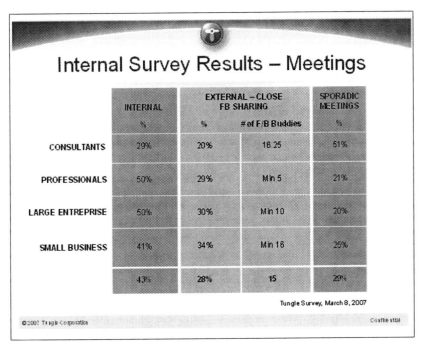

Internal Survey Results – Meetings

	INTERNAL %	EXTERNAL – CLOSE FB SHARING %	# of F/B Buddies	SPORADIC MEETINGS %
CONSULTANTS	29%	20%	16.25	51%
PROFESSIONALS	50%	29%	Min 5	21%
LARGE ENTREPRISE	50%	30%	Min 10	20%
SMALL BUSINESS	41%	34%	Min 16	25%
	43%	28%	15	29%

Tungle Survey, March 8, 2007

© 2007 Tungle Corporation   Confidential

Figure 18: Tungle Survey Results about Meetings

A survey Tungle conducted in March of this year (see Figure 18) showed that about 40% of meetings are scheduled with internal people, 30% outside the firewall with known people, and 30% more ad-hoc meetings (outside the firewall) and possibly with people you don't know.

In their beta, Tungle focuses on meetings for the first 70%, that is, with people you know and with whom you can set up the meeting in advance. When it moves out of beta this fall, it will offer tools to help address the other 30% of meetings (ad-hoc meetings with those you may not know well and do not want to have looking at your calendar).

Other Options

iPolipo

iPolipo, is one of the only online meeting scheduling service that does not use e-mail to schedule meetings. iPolipo focuses on setting up 1-to-1 meetings (only), which they believe is the majority of meetings (actually CS research shows that ≥90% of all web meetings are under 5 people). iPolipo research shows that on average it took 5-7 e-mails to set up a 1-to-1 meeting. Their philosophy focuses first on do you want to meet with this person, rather than do I have common free time to meet with them (more like TimeBridge).

Often you will agree to a meeting based on the other person's role (i.e., your wife, boss, colleague, etc.). If it is my wife, she should see a very different free/busy calendar than a client or prospect would. Through an Outlook plug-in, you can add specific people to each of the groups you create.

Everyone who wants to share their calendar has to be a member of iPolipo (have their own account). In general, the people they are scheduling meetings with do not need to be an iPolipo user, because there is the option of setting up a limited time invite for people that are not iPolipo users. A good example of this is, is a one-time-only-and-ever "meeting" with the city electrical inspector to have your new wiring looked at.

Obviously anyone can have an iPolipo account, but you don't have to have one to use the system. People that set up meetings with other specific users on a regular basis generally ask them to become an iPolipo user too. Free/Available meeting times are published to the iPolipo web site, so others who want to meet with another iPolipo user can visit the site and sees what times are available for a meeting.

Calgoo

Calgoo is the Java-based application that syncs up your online and offline calendars (beta) and now is a public download. With the update comes support for iCal, Microsoft Outlook, and both tiers of Google Applications (free and premiere). It's also undergone a face-lift that looks like Apple's iCal married Microsoft's Outlook. Calgoo does require a small download, but what is nice is that you can create appointments and schedule your Google Calendar without going online. The next time you are able to connect, Calgoo will sync up your changes.

Calgoo released Calgoo Apps 1.0, the first production release of its online and offline calendaring application. Calgoo Apps is the only calendaring solution that enables smooth synchronization and visualization of multiple calendars, allowing users to manage tasks, coordinate events, and direct their schedules through the use of only one program. Calgoo Apps's online/offline feature maximizes users' productivity by allowing them to input information into their calendar while offline and upload the new data when logged online. In addition, with the ability to synchronize Outlook and Google calendar, users can view colleagues' availability and coordinate activities, plan and book meetings and events with clients, partners, and family, and coordinate their work, home and social lives.

Time and Avatars Wait for No Man

As you can see, there has been great progress in using Web 2.0 technologies to address complex time issues. Another way to manage some of these issues is to have your avatar—an online representative of you—take the meeting.

6 Collaboration 2.5

> *"Whatever is experienced, whatever happens, know that this **Avatar** willed it so. There is no force on earth which can delay for an instant the mission for which this **Avatar** has come. You are all sacred souls and you will have your parts to play in the unfolding drama of the new Golden Age, which is coming."*—Sri Sathya Sai Baba

Web 3.0 promises to be the semantic web populated with intelligent agents. Yet many still have trouble just coordinating our calendars, indicating that Web 3.0 is a few years off. Letting go of mundane practicality for just a moment, a number of new technologies are shifting the experience of collaboration from the familiar 2-D (two dimensional) environments to virtual worlds where online collaboration appears to take place in 3-D (three dimensional). Provided here is the overview of offerings that fall into this realm. Since these realms are not yet part of the semantic web, but more advanced than the 2-D web, the only logical moniker would be: Collaboration 2.5.

Avatars and Virtual Worlds

Yahoo! has offered up free avatars for almost two years, but these caricatures can't be personalized to reflect what a good number of the application's users actually look like. They are geared toward the young, fit, fashionable set. For good or bad, there are no options to outfit your avatar with a comb-over, beer gut, or a double chin. These blinking, slightly emotive characters can only be used within the Yahoo! network.

Similarly, Palo Alto, California-based chat startup IMVU also offers avatars. Like Yahoo, they are 3-D characters you create to represent yourself. However, these avatars can't be used on other instant-messaging systems.

Sophia's Garden Foundation, Healing in Community™ Online (HICO), is a Web-based survival kit for families of kids with chronic or terminal illnesses. They are breaking new ground in the health care world with their 3-D environment. Karen Herzog, the Director, wanted to investigate a number of avatar-related tools including SitePal™ and Voki. Both these Oddcast™ tools enable the creation and embedding of customized animated characters within web pages, blogs, social networks, e-mails, ad banners, and Flash movies.

Voki is a free social-network platform for creating avatars, and employs an interesting viral marketing technique (some premium services may be offered in the future). SitePal offers a variety of subscription options that should suit everyone from the consumer and small business to the Fortune 1000 enterprise. A bronze level subscription to SitePal is $10/month, while the VHost Workshop™ (where multiple people can contribute to a character or brand for the enterprise) is $50,000. VHost is a brand-specific consumer-facing application that Oddcast's clients deploy to enable their visitors to customize their own VHost™ characters and messages, and publish them to galleries or e-mail them to friends. Whatever you choose, they all use the same basic avatar creation technology as well as Adobe Flash technology, with the different offerings just having more and different bells and whistles.

According to Oddcast's web site, "Any non-technical user can create and update characters, backgrounds, and audio messages effortlessly, without touching the underlying code. Basic HTML and Java programmers can utilize the VHost Studio's APIs to create advanced interactions with users based on their rollovers, clicks, and browser cookies." Avatars can be placed on your web site (with a code snippet of HTML) or in a TypePad or Blogger blog, or even on individual Facebook pages.

For HICO, Karen wanted to create an avatar that would introduce people to the site and help them with what they were trying to do. It only took a few minutes for her to create several different avatars on Voki. Here is a link to one of Karen's avatars:

http://tinyurl.com/yux2c8

Karen also looked at the VHost E-Learning Suite™ ($33,000) because it offers Simulation Maker™, FAQ Maker™, and Quiz Maker™ to support role playing, inter-active help, and assessments, respectively, which will be an integral part of the HICO site.

Building Your Avatar

When creating your Voki avatar, there are four steps to customize and publish it. The first step is to pick an avatar from an existing scene (you can use any avatars you have already created) as your template and begin to edit it or create one from scratch. Karen chose to create one from scratch, and she got to choose from seven general different character styles. Then she chose gender (M, F), once that was chosen she got to choose hair length and color, skin color, etc., even clothing, and bling. With each choice, you get different general styles and characteristics to choose from.

Then you need to choose the background for your avatar (step 2). You can choose one of their general backgrounds which are set up in a variety of categories (Travel, Outdoors, etc.), or you can upload your own picture to be the background. However, when Karen tried to upload a photo (JPEG), it did not work.

Once you have created the look of your avatar, then you need to give it a voice (step 3). The easiest way is to phone in what you want the avatar to say, much like creating a voice mail recording. However, you can also use the microphone on your computer, type your message and have it converted to speech or even upload an audio file (wav, mp3, wma, pcm).

Finally (step 4) you need to create a theme for the player. Once you have created your avatar on Voki, you can customize the message and send it by e-mail to a specific person (viral marketing) or have a general one for everyone to see (there are hundreds on the site). Voki users can also send each other's Voki readable on the site (social networking) and send it to your Voki avatar that is also an inter-system address.

The business model for SitePal and VHost is pretty clear, but we are not sure what the Voki business model will be. Since it focuses on social networking, it might be some sort of ad-based revenue and premium services (special items or characters and downloading to mobile phones) once the site is out of the alpha and beta stages and in production. A branding strategy is the Voki Partner Program, which "allows communities and social networks to enable their users to create personalized, speaking avatars, and publish them to web pages and applications. Partners are provided with the ability to integrate the user-generated avatars into their own platform, through a simple and secure API." For now, the Voki partner program is free to qualifying communities and social networks.

Putting Oddcast to Work

In Figure 19, you can see a Nurse/Coach avatar for one of the more medical parts of the HICO community.

The avatars in HICO are asynchronous avatars, and like an e-mail message, are always there for you to play with and allow for information gathering and guidance. However, because HICO is being developed in Qwaq (a 3-D collaborative environment), there are also Qwaq avatars, which can be called synchronous avatars since they are a real-time representation of a person in the Qwaq environment.

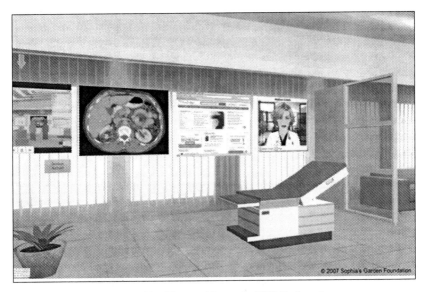

Figure 19: Nurse/Coach HICO Avatar

Virtual Worlds and 3-D Collaborative Environments

Tixio, a 3-D collaborative environment from France, uses avatars to represent people in a common (collaborative) space. Comverse Technology has announced an avatar service called "Klonies," designed solely for mobile services, but the product has yet to launch in the U.S.

Meez allows users to create caricatures of their own selves and then use that avatar wherever they want. Meez has received over $4 million in venture funding. This free, Web-based service offers thousands of facial and costume combinations, but Meez CEO Sean Ryan plans to make money by offering users the chance to have their avatars wear licensed brands, like Major League Baseball and National Hockey League jerseys, and premium clothing designs for a fee. Pricing should be similar to the cost of ring tones or wallpaper downloads. Ryan says Meez doesn't yet allow users to move avatars to their phones but that is in their plan.

Second Life is a three-dimensional digital world in which players can do just about anything: Create an avatar that acts as an online alter-ego, fly around landscapes dotted with dance clubs and gardens, and socialize via text messaging with friends via avatar interactions. The population inside Second Life has grown eightfold between 2005 and 2006. At this point, 20,000 "residents," as they are known, call it a second home. The game is drawing legions of eager players and big bucks from VCs who see hard profits in a booming fantasy world and are taking avatars a step further by supporting a whole virtual economy based on it.

Recently, because Second Life opened up its registration (before you needed a credit card to sign up), it has jumped from 2.5 million registered users to almost 8 million registered users in 9 months. However, if you do go on the site, usually only about 10% of the registered users are online at any one time, and only about 10% of those are active users. Many in Second Life are experimenting with being virtual gangster/rappers and trying unusual sex acts.

Second Life is a whole economy in itself, and even has a daily report showing the exchange rate of Linden dollars (Linden Labs makes Second Life) to U.S. dollars. It also shows how many dollars have been exchanged each day (see Figure 20).

Total Residents:	7,703,759
Logged In Last 60 Days:	1,766,092
Online Now:	38,787
US$ Spent Last 24h:	$1,811,830

Figure 20: A Day in Second Life

Second Life is just one of the many "Massively Multiplayer Online Role-Playing Games" or MMORPGs. The top-seller in this category, *World of Warcraft* from Vivendi's Blizzard Entertainment unit, is probably the best known with more than 8 million players, each of whom pays $15 a month. Unlike *World of Warcraft*, where players go on quests and slay monsters, participants in Second Life create their own reality, such as one was able to do with the popular Sims game series.

EverQuest, with more than 450,000 players worldwide, also has its own internal economy in which players' trade virtual goods that they generate as they play. They can even use the game's token currency—platinum pieces. Killing creatures for their treasure is another popular approach to acquiring wealth. The longer one plays, the more powerful one gets. Some who have been playing since its launch in 1999, own entire virtual castles filled with treasures from their quests.

Interestingly, EverQuest's *virtual* economy has overlapped with the *actual* economy; An EverQuest player might tire of the game and decide to sell off her characters or virtual possessions on an on-line auction site such as eBay. A *Belt of the Great Turtle* or a *Robe of Primordial Waters* might fetch as much as 40 *real US dollars;* powerful characters could go for several hundred or more. Sometimes people sell off 500,000-fold bags of platinum pieces for as much as $1,000. Based on the calculations of one out-of-work economist a "platinum piece" was worth about one U.S. penny and, on average, an EverQuest player was making about $3.50/ hour.

In these virtual worlds, individuals often team up to accomplish tasks or overtake a competitor and steal his goods. Detailed menus allow you to create everything from avatar clothes, to buildings, to games that are played inside the virtual world. Each "resident" of a virtual world is like an annuity, the longer they subscribe and the more complex their character becomes the greater their value and the more tightly hooked into the subscription service they become.

However, online gaming is not just fun and games. It is also being recognized for its abilities as a *good training tool* for enhancing cognition, simulations of difficult situations, decision making, leadership training, military training, increasing perception, problem solving, social communication, and strategic analysis.

Big retailers are using online games to promote new products. Chrysler, for instance, created a game to promote its new Wrangler Rubicon that reportedly generated fourteen percent of the vehicle's initial orders. The U.S. Army recently spent more than $7 million on a suite of games to support the increasingly difficult task of signing on 120,000 new soldiers each year. The results are impressive. Since July 4th, 2002, 1.2 million registrants played 55 million game missions for an average of 10 minutes each; 758,584 players completed the game's basic-training component; Web site hits went from 30,000 hits per day pre-game launch to half a million post-launch.

According to Linden Labs, people with Asperger's Syndrome (a mild form of autism that affects approximately 5 in 1000 school-aged children, often getting in the way of social interactions) can use avatars to practice social interactions and get better at real-life social interactions.

At some point, we may re-evaluate what we define as "actual" versus "virtual life and work," as distributed networked life and work become the prevailing way of interacting. In fact, self-service technology tools that allow for the creation of one's own unique interactive environments are on the rise. As they become more sophisticated on the server side (back end) and easier for the end-user (front end) to use, the ability to create, re-invent and transform interactive environments to suite one's lifestyle, work style, mood or other variables will become as easy as deciding what you'll wear or how you'll decorate your room (e.g., like creating an avatar).

A recent Business Week article entitled "Just Ahead: The Web as a Virtual World" posits the ability to not only create an avatar for yourself, but the ability of that avatar to seamlessly move from one virtual environment to another.[16] This would require that technical standards be established which would make the Internet a galaxy of connected virtual worlds (moving them more into the area of the Semantic Web). The Web3D consortium hopes to have this worked out within 18 months through a shared file format called X3D. X3D will be a just-in-time standard since an industry analyst estimates that by 2011 80% of Internet users and major companies will have avatars.[17]

---

16. Just Ahead: The Web as a Virtual World, *Business Week*, http://tinyurl.com/2m6nsc, August 13, 2007.

Multiverse Network, Inc. that creates a platform for 3-D virtual worlds already allows avatars to move from one world to the next, and because these tools are free there are about 200 different virtual worlds being developed on the Multiverse platform. To give you a better idea of the explosion in virtual worlds I have compiled a list below:

Doppleganger; Kaneva; Meez, Active Worlds; Coke Studios; Club Penguin; Cybertown; Disney's Toontown; Dreamville; Dubit; Habbo Hotel; The Manor; Mokitown; Moove; Muse; The Palace; Playdo; The Sims Online; Sora City; There; TowerChat; Traveler; Virtual Ibiza; Virtual Magic Kingdom; Voodoo Chat; VPchat; VZones; whyrobbierocks; Whyville; Worlds.com; Yohoho! Puzzle Pirates; Gaia Online. All of these worlds are reviewed at: Virtual Worlds Review.

If you want a more complete list, Virtual Worlds News provides one here:

http://tinyurl.com/24ocxg

3-D Collaborative Environments

Recently, with Eilif Trondsen (of SRI Consulting BI [business intelligence]) in tow, we had the chance to see two 3-D collaborative environments that are early on in their development. The first is Qwaq, which is a commercial implementation of the Croquet Project (open source), and the second is Sun Lab's Wonderland, which is developed in Java, and is currently being released into open source.

Qwaq

The Croquet Project is an international effort to promote the continued development of Croquet, a free software platform and network operating system for developing and delivering deeply collaborative multi-user online applications. It features a network architecture that supports communication, collaboration, resource sharing, and synchronous computation among multiple users. Croquet provides a

---

17. Mitch Wagner, *InformationWeek*, April 26, 2007.

flexible framework in which most user interface concepts can be proto-typed and deployed to create powerful and highly collaborative multi-user 2-D and 3-D applications and simulations. Croquet can be used to construct highly scalable collaborative data visualizations, virtual learning, and problem solving environments, wikis, online gaming environments (MMORPGs), and privately maintained and in-terconnected multi-user virtual environments.

The Croquet Project now has a commercial implementation in Qwaq (which is now in early general release). Qwaq is a 3-D collaborative environment that is based on an object-oriented model that gives it many powerful features for collaboration.

According to the Qwaq website, Qwaq has these characteristics:

Designed for Collaboration

Qwaq Forums is designed for collaboration. Whether you are working internally with other team members and groups, or need to collaborate with supply chain partners or customers, Qwaq Forums have powerful features that simplify setting up and working in highly collaborative environments.

- *Content. Content is easily made available to users; simply drag and drop content from your local folders or desktop into Qwaq Forums and it will be automatically uploaded and made available to other users. Using Qwaq Multi-Share,™ multiple users can edit content together within a virtual space. Once a work item is completed, content can be saved to your local desktop or folders for further processing.*

- *Presence. Unlike traditional 2-D collaboration environments, Qwaq Forums' 3-D environment provides strong feedback on where users are focusing and what users are working on. Using avatars and a unique "laser pointer" makes it easy to see where people are, what they are looking at, what content they are editing, and how they are using applications. In combination with Qwaq Forums' built-in high fidelity VoIP and text chat, users have a highly immersive environment and important social cues that help them work more effectively.*

- **Context.** A Qwaq Forums workspace provides a simple way to link and associate content. Whether using drag-and-drop to link virtual spaces or simply choosing the spatial relationship between content in an existing space, users can establish areas of focus for collaboration.

- **Persistence.** The virtual spaces in Qwaq Forums are designed to be dynamic and evolving. Users can save the state of a Qwaq Forums virtual space at any time. The saved state includes any editing made by users to documents or content in the space; for example, if you had been working on a budgeting spreadsheet, any changes you and other users made to that spreadsheet would be saved along with the rest of the state of the virtual space. This capability provides a powerful way for users to work on projects that cannot be completed in one session and allows them to leave incremental work updates for each other when working asynchronously.

Powerful End User Features

- Simple virtual workspace creation. Create meeting rooms, offices, lab rooms or other indoor spaces from existing room templates. The templates provide ready-to-use rooms that can be used right away or further customized. Use the Qwaq Virtual Campus™ to create outdoor spaces. All spaces can be linked together using drag and drop commands.

- Drag and drop content import. Share Microsoft Office documents created with Word, PowerPoint and Excel; Adobe PDF files, images, and even 3-D content by dragging from local folders into a Qwaq Forums virtual workspace.

- Qwaq Multi-Share™. Qwaq's unique fine-grained sharing control lets multiple users edit a document or use an application GUI in an intuitive manner at the same time. All users see edits in real-time.

Qwaq Forums Architecture Highlights

- Scalable Peer-to-Peer architecture for user Interactions.

- Built-in wide area VoIP and text chat.

- *Built-in data encryption: all traffic between peers is encrypted to ensure privacy.*

- *Option to have Qwaq Host or to Self-Host behind your firewall.*

- *Open standards based: uses Croquet for platform and Python for scripting. Supports numerous document types for user import and export.*

However, Qwaq does require a PC that is "Vista" capable, with enough CPU and graphics processing power, as well as a good broadband connection, to make working in the environment more than an exercise in frustration (Sun's environment also requires a reasonable amount of processing power, the more objects in the environment, the more graphics processing power is needed). I had a Dell Latitude, Pentium 4, 2 GHz, with 1 GB of RAM and had to move to a new Dell Vostro 1500 laptop with an Intel Core 2 Duo processor at 2.2 GHz with 4 GB of RAM and an NVIDIA graphics card with 256 MB RAM on it. It work very well in 3-D environments and there was very little lag (attributable to the network) with regard to the movement of avatars in the environment, or viewing and sharing any content in any of the rooms we built as part of the HICO project.

Because it is a very new environment, it still is not as user friendly as it could be, but the Qwaq team is working on that. Within a year or so, when there are more computers with the power and connection speeds needed for Qwaq it will become a popular collaborative environment.

The metaphor for Qwaq is a bit different than what you may be familiar with, and with your avatar, navigation takes a bit of getting used to. You can jump to a named place through a drop down menu or you can walk your avatar over to a specific screen. As in many 3-D environments, you also have different points of view.

Adding content also takes some getting used to. Although Qwaq supports drag-and-drop of content from your desktop or a web site into a file (rolodex) or a screen (for viewing) the navigation is non-standard and does take some getting used to. What is nice about this environment is that it mostly resides on your desktop (about a 50 MB download) and it really is only passing tokens (about avatar movement, screen changes, etc.) to the Qwaq server. With the token passing everyone's image in the same room (or forum) is synchronized through the server pretty much in real-time (depending on the speed of your computer, connection speed, and the load on the server). This architecture is both a space and time saver for those using the environment.

Some of the advantages of the shared content feature are that others in the room can see the document (or web page or multi-media object) you are showing, and can even work with you on editing it. Another advantage of Qwaq is persistence and that the document really stays on your desktop (and in your Qwaq Forum) and this alleviates worrying about some of the copyright and security issues that most VTS (Virtual Team Spaces) have.

Although at the time Qwaq was tested, the user had to invoke a menu option to see who else was in the room with you, in the future that window will pop-up automatically so that an individual will always know who else is there, which is a valuable aid in social interactions with other users. Figure 21 shows a standard room, with the participants and the ability to share a variety of different content types with people in the room. The orange figure is a simplistic avatar.

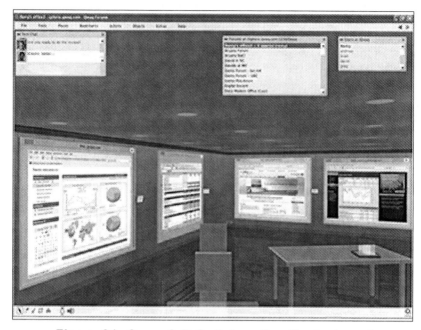

Figure 21: Qwaq 3-D Collaborative Environment

In Qwaq, some graphics objects require much more processing power than others, and some objects can be simplified without losing their identity but can be much more thrifty (in terms of graphical processing). Hopefully, in the future Qwaq will offer a palette of objects that you can use to decorate an office or a room, and you can just drag and drop them in, change the color or shape, elongate them, etc. The other issue is getting them to be in the room in a reasonable way, so that the bed is on the floor, not floating an inch or two above it, or that it is square with the wall, etc. An optional snap-to grid would help make this easier for users who are not graphic artists to populate the room with objects.

Qwaq is oriented towards business users rather than the hoards of consumers relegated to things such as Second Life. There is a more robust security model in both Owaq and Wonderland, which is positioned the same way.

Once you get used to the navigation and creating objects (in our case, using Google Sketch-up) in Qwaq the environment feels more "natural." The collaboration is relatively easy: you post a document on a board and everyone in the room can see and interact with it. This is very powerful, and other 2-D collaborative environments should be envious of these features. Some non-technical people who saw Qwaq felt that it was far too much like a 3-D gaming environment (and most mentioned Second Life).

Exploding Pigs and Intellectual Capital

Virtual worlds and 3-D collaborative environments are very hot right now and there has been an explosion of them in the last 6 months. With Second Life (which is the most well known) 3-D environments jumped to 7 million residents (from about 2.5 million) in a 9-month period, which obviously got everyone's attention. Typically, there are about 40,000 people on-line on Second Life at any one time.

However, Second Life has issues of its own. Although it has released the client as an open source, it has not yet released the server as open source. This makes intellectual property a problem. For example, say an individual creates clothes for an avatar in Second Life and sells them (and many people do). Now say this same individual gets kicked out of Second Life. Even though it was the specific individual who created the clothing they are unable to use them in another environment, and this is true of any intellectual property that they might've developed.

The second problem in Second Life is security. You could be in a business meeting for instance: in a Second Life room and some 12-year-old can send a pig through the wall of your room, which, upon entering, explodes, disturbing the meeting (and delighting the 12-year-old). However, this can only happen if you are on the Second Life Island. Most serious businesses (like IBM, Cisco, Intel, etc.) have bought their own islands (a good source of revenue for Second Life) and limit the access to the island... so no exploding pigs!

The third big problem is scalability. All of the 3-D environments are limited by the complexity of the environment; in Second Life it is the number of polygons in the area covered by the server. In Wonderland and Qwaq, it is the number and complexity of the objects in the room that determines the number of people and reaction times.

The fourth big problem with Second Life is that you can't currently display a web page or use a white board and so it is not as capable a collaborative environment as Qwaq which was built for that purpose.

All of the 3-D environments mentioned, because they are early versions, seem to have scalability and other issues based on the 3-D rendering and processing required. Second Life, being the most popular will probably have to re-architect first to deal with this scalability issue. Taking all these limitations into account and the fact that it is much cheaper "to move bits than butts" one wonders what your "carbon footprint" in Second Life is?

Welcome to Wonderland

In July, word began to circulate about Sun Microsystems' new virtual collaborative environment called Wonderland, positioned for businesses and written in Java. This environment is even younger than Qwaq (the Wonderland project began in January 2007) and came from Dave Douglas, the VP of Eco-responsibility at Sun, when he said "the next building Sun makes should be a virtual one." So the MPK20 project was born (MPK 20 stands for Menlo Park Campus building #20. There are 19 physical buildings on the campus).

Wonderland is seen as the client side of the project and MPK20 is a specific research project to see how these 3-D environments can be used internally at Sun in a work environment.

"Project Wonderland is a 3-D scene manager for creating collaborative virtual worlds. Within those worlds, users can communicate with high-fidelity, immersive audio and can share live applications such as web browsers, OpenOffice documents, and games.

The vision for this multi-user virtual environment is to provide an environment that is robust enough in terms of security, scalability, reliability, and functionality that organizations can rely on as a place to conduct real business. Organizations should be able to use Wonderland to create a virtual presence to better communicate with customers, partners, and employees. Individuals should be able to do their real work within a virtual world, eliminating the need for a separate collaboration tool when they wish to work together with others. Individuals should also be able to tailor portions of the world to adapt to their work needs and to express their personal style. The types of collaborations that can happen within the space will eventually include audio communication, live desktop applications of all kinds, and collaborative creation of world content (both graphical and procedural).

One important goal of the project is for the environment to be completely extensible. Developers and graphic artists can extend the functionality to create entire new worlds, new features in existing worlds, or new behaviors for objects and avatars. The art path for Wonderland is also open. The eventual goal is to support content creation within the world, but in the shorter term, the goal is to support importing art from open source 3-D content creation tools as well as professional 3-D modeling and animation applications."

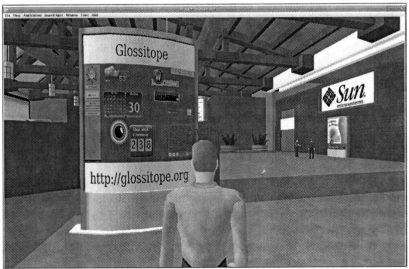

***Figure 22: A View into the Sun Wonderland Environment
(including Avatar)***

In the demo we saw, all the windows were hard coded (which will be fixed in the near future) and anyone in the environment that is an Avatar has their name above their head (see Figure 22), others in the environment are called "sims" and do not have a real person attached to them. The ability to show multiple types of information on a variety of "panels" (see Figure 23) is also a great advantage in collaborating on a complex project and allows you (or your avatar) to refer to multiple objects without having to flip back and forth between documents.

Figure 23: Showing Multiple Panels of
Information/Applications in a Wonderland Room

Size Counts

Wonderland rooms don't have to be static in size, shape, or any other metric and can be created to reflect their use, for example, you can create a small room for a two person meeting, and a larger room for a multi-person conference. The room size can be an indicator of the amount of content in the room (i.e., if you go into a project room that has hundreds of documents it would be larger than a project room with only a few documents, and that way, you could tell the size of the project as soon as you stepped into the room). It would also be useful if (as in Qwaq) a presence list of those in the room were posted so that it could be seen immediately upon entering the room.

Wonderland avoids the exploding pig problem by not having 12-year-olds use it and using an LDAP authentication security model. It also uses the Sun Voice technology to offer high quality sound so that if you are near a person talking it is louder and as your avatar moves further away the talking gets softer. This also allows you to have multiple simultaneous conversations in one room (think *cocktail party*).

Sun will try to extend Wonderland features to work with devices less capable than a computer, and should be able to support telephones (PSTN) and cell phone/PDAs in the near future. One nice thing about Wonderland is that it is all cached on your PC, so that if you are disconnected you can still work in the environment and sync up again once you are back on line.

Without getting too technical, where is this taking us? The obvious answer is to an environment that gives us more than we would have in a F2F meeting, such as: more freedom of movement (you can fly or teleport in a 3-D environment), more information at a glance (look at the walls in Qwaq or Wonderland), and more information about each other and our interactions with each other. These new environments for collaboration or business interactions, I call *augmented environments*.

Augmented Environments

Everyone in the demo agreed that there was limited expression and gestures from the avatars in the room, and if you have ever played in Second Life, doing these things, which are "natural" in a F2F meeting, can be difficult in these collaborative environments. Because the feedback would not be the same as if involved in a F2F, people are simply unwilling to talk about emotional or personal issues in these environments (research done by Nichole Yankelovich at Sun Labs).[18] This is because most individuals do not trust that they will get appropriate feedback for these sensitive issues in such environments.

---

18. Personal Conversation with Nichole Yankelovich at a Sun Labs briefing on Wonderland, May 2007.

What is needed is an augmented virtual meeting environment where everyone would be able to get more (and different) information than in a F2F meeting.

There are a number of groups working on augmented environments, and Christine Perey, who works with the AMI Consortium, a multi-disciplinary research network in Europe, wrote an article about the future of business meetings, which looks at an experimental augmented environment. The AMI Consortium user interface architecture for navigating and browsing multimedia meetings is called JFerret. It is used to browse rich meeting archives that are stored with related metadata in a database. It is a Java-based architecture supporting plug-ins (29 currently).

The JFerret browser combines the appropriate metadata and raw data in a unified view on the user's screen. As you can see from figure 24 below, those in the meeting are getting a lot more data about the others in the meeting (local or remote) than they would if they were just in a F2F meeting. It is this kind of augmented environment that I believe meetings in 3-D spaces will evolve to.

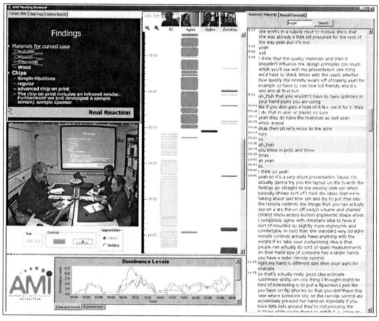

Figure 24: JFerret is a Java-Based, Browser Architecture for Meetings

Not only do they need to provide more information than one would get in a normal F2F meeting, but they need to do it in an easier way, so that it does not take a technical expert to take part in one of these meetings. In this case simplicity means only a few clicks: a click to get into the 3-D environment and into your default room, a click to see who else is there, a click to share an object or document, and a click to interact with others in the environment. Good stereo audio gives clues on location in the environment, while augmented information can let you know who is paying attention, what their real reactions are to what you're saying or showing, and statistics on how others are perceiving you (in real time).

For the "Net Geners" (those in their 20's and 30's) who have grown up with computers (as opposed to Baby Boomers) and are thought to have this mythical ability to pay attention to multiple things on the computer and in their real environments, these 3-D collaborative environments might seem like a natural progression in the evolution of "things to pay attention to." For these time slicing individuals the next step would be to run multiple avatars in the same meeting, and then multiple avatars in multiple meetings. Think of it, being able to be in two places at once, which in a way would be transcending the laws of physics, and would allow for more meetings in a day, hour, or week.

It is not a guarantee that "Net Geners" have a mythical ability to do "continuous partial attention," (more on this in our online community). Even with this ability it might not be enough to enable someone to participate in multiple simultaneous meetings without having some kind of augmentation of their own. That would require intelligent agents or some other Web 3.0 technologies of Web 3.0, but that is another story.

Social Networks and Virtual Worlds

A friend once said "I had to quit all the social networks I was in, just to have enough time to have dinner with friends every once in a while."

Social networks like LinkedIn, Facebook, and MySpace are the hottest ticket on the Internet right now. It is easy to get venture capital for them and they exemplify the second order effect of technology in that they focus on both content and interaction between individuals and groups. With Facebook opening up its API to outside developers in the spring of 2007, over 7000 add-on applications are now available on Facebook. Tools like Jaxtr allow Facebook users to call each other over VoIP from their computers with the click of a button.

But environments like Second Life are also looking at opening up their APIs to outside developers. Imagine if Second Life were mashed-up with Facebook, the user could interact with some of their Facebook friends in a specific environment in a virtual world.

Let's say many of your friends on Facebook are from College and you went to Stanford. You could create a group on Facebook for Stanford Graduates, but it would be a lot cooler to create a virtual world in Second Life or Multiverse that looked like the Stanford campus, and then alumni events could take place in a virtual Stanford as well as in the real world, sometimes even simultaneously. It seems some developers already expect this evolution to take place rather quickly, and a year old company by the name of Areae based in San Diego, is building a virtual world that it claims will integrate more easily with other Web sites by design.

OpenSocial

Google has recently announced OpenSocial, which provides a common set of APIs for social applications across multiple websites. With standard JavaScript and HTML, developers can create applications that access a social network's friends and updates feeds. OpenSocial is based on Google Gadgets (a type of widget) and allows these applications to work on any social networks (called "hosts") that choose to participate. OpenSocial is a set of three common APIs, defined by Google with input from partners that allow developers to access core functions and information at social networks:

- Profile Information (user data)
- Friends Information (social graph)
- Activities (things that happen, News Feed type stuff)

This seems to be part of Google's answer to Facebook. Unlike Facebook, OpenSocial does not have its own markup language (Facebook requires the use of FBML for security reasons, but it also makes code unusable outside of Facebook). Instead, developers use normal JavaScript and html (and can embed Flash elements). The benefit of the Google approach is that developers can use much of their existing front end code and simply tailor it slightly for OpenSocial, so creating applications is even easier than on Facebook.

At its launch on October 30th, two categories of partners announced with Google: hosts and developers. Hosts are the participating social networks, and include Orkut, Salesforce, LinkedIn, Ning, Hi5, Plaxo, Friendster, Viadeo, Oracle, NewsGator and MySpace. Developers include Flixster, iLike, RockYou and Slide.

Time will only tell if this was a great marketing move by Google or red herring for developers.

7 Virtual Team Challenges

"Only as a warrior can one withstand the path of knowledge. A warrior cannot complain or regret anything. His life is an endless challenge, and challenges cannot possibly be good or bad. Challenges are simply challenges."
—Carlos Castaneda

Types of Virtual Teams

Depending on the nature of the work, a team comes together to do and the types of organization they work for/with, virtual teams fall into seven basic types:

- **Networked Teams** consist of individuals who collaborate to achieve a common goal or purpose; membership is frequently diffuse and fluid.

- **Parallel Teams** work over a short term to develop recommendations for an improvement in a process or system; have a distinct membership.

- **Project or Product-Development Teams** conduct projects for users or customers for a defined period. Tasks are usually non-routine, and the results are specific and measurable; teams have decision-making authority.

- **Work or Production Teams** perform regular and ongoing work usually in one function; clearly defined membership.

- **Service Teams** support customers or the internal organization (typically) in a service/technical support role around the clock.

- **Management Teams** work collaboratively on a daily basis within a functional division of a corporation.

- **Action Teams** offer immediate responses (typically) activated in emergency situations.

Teamwork joins people and process together to divide the labor and creatively collaborate to produce a set of desired results. Whether the members of a team come together around a table or meet across the ether, the most frequent challenges that emerge in developing strong and productive teams are:

- Solid, effective communication
- Strong team leadership
- Development of shared understanding, purpose or commitment
- Bridging differences and building trust

As humans, when initially meeting someone in person, assessments are made that establish the beginning of bond, or a red flag of distrust: do they look us in the eye, is their handshake firm, do they sound confident and believable…do they smell right? We also base our sense of trust on commonalities. On the way to a co-located meeting, for example, a casual conversation in the hallway might yield answers to questions of commonality: Do we like the same kinds of sports or do we share the same hobbies? Do we have similar family structures and responsibilities? Do we have similar work or educational experiences?

Paraphrasing John Katzenbach and Douglas Smith from their book, *The Wisdom of Teams: Creating the High-Performance Organization*, a team is a small number of people (from 2 to 25, but not more than 25 or they break up into sub-groups). They have complementary skills (of three types: technical or functional expertise, problem-solving and decision-making, or interpersonal), and are committed to a common purpose, an established set of performance goals, and an agreed upon approach for which they hold themselves mutually accountable. It is the mutual accountability that is seen as the actual turning point, the point at which a set of individuals becomes a team.[19]

The traditional concept of a team is a group of people working together toward a shared set of goals. In the past, "together" generally meant physically close by.

Distributed Teams

When it comes to meeting the complexity of modern-day projects, achieving clarity and communicating effectively about individual accountability, which seems simple, can be quite challenging. This is especially true when teams comprise members from different cultures (even within the same organization or country) or speak different languages (or different dialects of the same language, say, British versus American English or English as a second language.)

In their 1994 book *GlobalWork: Bridging Distance, Culture & Time*, Mary O'Hara Devereaux and Robert Johansen, emerging-technology researchers with The Institute for the Future, noted a shift in the way cultural diversity is being regarded by organizations in the new global world of work:

"Historically businesses have viewed diversity as a chronic problem that had to be minimized and managed. The new challenge of global-ization represents an opportunity to take a radically different approach: one that embraces diversity in ways that allow business to grow and profit from the many dramatically different cultural qualities that char-acterize most of our communities and organizations."

---

19. John Katzenbach and Douglas Smith, *The Wisdom of Teams: Creating the High-Performance Organization* (Boston: Harvard Business School Press, 1993).

Deveraux and Johansen go on to challenge leaders to find ways to shift the mindset, turning diversity from a problem to an advantage.[20]

In face-to-face team environments, bonds are generally established in casual interactions that occur randomly—a discussion about the weekend's events while getting coffee, an outing to a local watering hole with a group of teammates after work, the sharing of baby pictures, or replaying the highlights of a sporting event while waiting for a meeting to get started. These activities include sharing hand gestures, facial expressions, props and other here-and-now objects, and other phenomena that are harder to recreate for members of distributed teams. But for team members to feel as though they are respected and that their contributions are both welcome and valued, these types of interactions must take place in some way.

Individuals on distributed teams are at some disadvantage in gathering the type of interpersonal information that comes from face-to-face interaction, which would help them better identify with the others on the team. These include cues that individuals frequently use to gauge another's reliability and competence such as: Does he look me in the eye when he talks? Does the smirk mean she's being sarcastic?

An interesting article in the May, 2004 Harvard Business Review about "Can Absence Make Teams Grow Stronger," also by Jessica Lipnak and Jeffrey Stamps (NetAge), looked at 54 teams across 26 companies and 15 industries, and noted 3 rules or best practices for these very distributed teams:

1. Exploit Diversity

2. Use Technology to simulate reality

3. Hold the team together[21]

---

20. Mary O'Hara Devereaux and Robert Johansen, *GlobalWork: Bridging Distance, Culture & Time* (New York: Jossey-Bass, 1994).
21. Jessica Lipnak and Jeffrey Stamps, *Can Absence Make Teams Grow Stronger* (Boston: Harvard Business Review, 2004)

Why Teams Fail

For teams to work together successfully, it is imperative that the team leader make sure that trust is forged in a deliberate and explicit way. It is, therefore, the team leader's responsibility to exhibit behaviors that engender and reinforce trust, including making social conversation, showing enthusiasm and responsiveness in team interactions (written and verbal) showing and rewarding individual initiative, demonstrating a predictable and consistent communication style and providing substantial and timely responses to inquiries.

On virtual teams, that initiative by the leader is unlikely to take place. One of the major reasons that many of today's teams are ineffective is that they overlook the implications of the obvious. People do not make accommodation for how different it really is when they and their colleagues no longer work face-to-face. Teams fail when they do not adjust to this new reality.

Alan and Deborah Slobodnik, principals of Options for Change, an organizational development learning group and consulting practice, have identified the following list for why teams fail:

- False Consensus
- Unresolved Overt Conflict
- Covert Conflict
- Rigid Hierarchy
- Weak Leadership
- Unrealistic Expectations
- Closure Avoidance
- Calcified Team Meetings
- Uneven Participation
- Lack of Mutual Accountability
- Left out Stakeholders
- Forgetting the Customer
- Adoration of Technology[22]

---

22. Alan and Deborah Slobodnik, Taking the Teeth Out of Team Traps, *The Systems Thinker*, Volume 10 Number 9, November 1999.

Teaming Challenges

The first step in understanding why a virtual team is not performing well is to understand that there are different types of potential conflicts:

- Cultural/language differences & fears

- Lack of trust (teammates, leaders, systems)

- Comfort/familiarity with existing tools and a perceived steep learning curve of new tool

- Inadequate team leadership to encourage full participation/communication

- Multiple tools in use; no clear commitment to one tool

- Insufficient IT support

These conflicts can be put into three basic categories:

- *Relationship conflicts* are an awareness of interpersonal differences. This category may include any manner of personality, language, or ethnic differences; hostility; or annoyance between individuals all of which can result in a lack of trust and have a negative impact on overall team productivity and morale.

- *Process conflicts* include disagreements regarding how to do the task or how to allocate resources. This category may include a discomfort with adapting to new tools. A perception that it will take too long to learn them, and/or a lack of trust in the choice or commitment to a particular tool. These disagreements could lead to a general lack of enthusiasm for full adoption.

- *Task or cognitive conflicts* are an awareness of differences in viewpoints pertaining to the goal/project.

Traditional notions of the workplace are giving way to more flexible ways to work. These changes involve the notion of place; the design of workplaces and infrastructure; the nature of outside business relationships; the tools that will be available to connect people, systems and information; and the leadership expectations necessary to make it all work. Technology will, of course, continue to play a key role in the way this is done. The new, flexible organization model will blend notions of place and design as the virtual team space continues to evolve. Below are some brief comments about these changes in society, technology, and the workplace.

Some predictable social trends include:

- Fully distributed educational infrastructure: education comes to the student and can be customized for each student
- Education to support the skills for development and maintenance of physical and e-communities
- The rise of guilds (could be online communities)
- Online voting
- The rise of the virtual committee!
- Defined by your communities (ex: gangs, colors, behaviors)
- Evolving social structures, not bounded by geography but rather by interest and connectedness (e.g., AARP-net) – political affinity groups

Visualizing Teams, Groups, and Value Networks

Collaborations—resulting from both philosophical changes and available technology—are changing the way we create community and define our affiliations and loyalties: Web 2.0 and social networks such as Friendster, MySpace, Tribe, LinkedIn, Plaxo, and a host of other applications (social networks) are creating significant new network affiliations through which teams of all kinds can form.

Social Network Analysis (SNA), Organizational Network Analysis (ONA) and Value Network Analysis (VNA) have been instrumental in deconstructing the nature, frequency, and value of relationships in social and organization structures, respectively. These models allow relationship elements to become an explicit part of applications. In turn, the relationships themselves can then be nurtured online between millions of people worldwide based on interest rather than proximity.

In her book, *The Future of Knowledge: Increasing Prosperity through Value Networks,* Verna Allee reflects on the idea of self-creation in organizations. Allee created HoloMaps®, which provides visual representations of the weighted value dynamics of tangibles and intangibles in an organizational network and reflects the unique and dynamic nature of that system. She is also a leading authority on VNA. Figure 25 shows an example of a value network map for tangible exchanges with a pharmaceutical company. In the figure, green solid lines and arrows depict tangible exchanges.

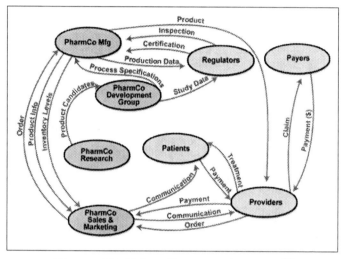

Figure 25: Value Network Example[23]

Rob Cross of the University of Virginia's McIntire School of Commerce has been concentrating his research on the organization rather than society at large. "Organizational network analysis provides an x-ray into the inner workings of an organization," explains Cross.

---

23. From Verna Allee: http://www.vernaallee.com.

"It is a powerful means of making invisible patterns of information flow and collaboration in strategically important groups visible.[24]

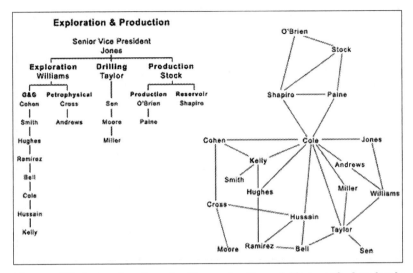

Figure 26: Introduction to Organizational Network Analysis

These tools provide a way to analyze teams, groups, and networks and give organizations enough information for structural, managerial and procedural changes that the company may need to make in order improve numerous areas. Some areas that could be affected are:

- Support alliances

- Leadership development

- Strategic decision making in top leadership networks

- Integration of networks across core processes

- Promoting innovation and productivity

---

24. Rob Cross, *Living in a Connected World*, http://www.robcross.org.

Rob Cross and Verna Allee both have contributed a great deal of understanding to the nature, spread and value of relationships from technological, sociological, political, and economic perspectives. We will continue to see reciprocal changes to social and organizational structures and technology as they continue to be reinvented by each other. Better understanding the impact of informal and virtual relationships can provide significant insight into the ways work actually gets done versus how an individual thinks it should.

Online Communities

I have been working with a group called CommunityXperts for several years, and their ideas and focus on creating online communities are very much in line with my philosophies, where the focus is always on the people and the relationships, and not the technology (which is just an enabler).

To make a distinction between an online community and a social network (and sometimes it is hard to tell the difference), one must look at the ties between individuals in the group. If they are strong, then it is probably a community, and if they are weak it is probably a social network. Another way to put this is "when you're not there and you are missed, it is a community. If you are not present and no one seems to notice then it is a social network."

Both the CommunityXperts team and I have worked with a variety of online communities and with all sorts of different software (yes it is getting better very rapidly), and we find that the success of these online communities is based on three factors. People join and stay in a community because they have an interest in the topic/content, enjoy interacting with the people in the community, and generally get something out of the community they can't get anywhere else. So when a community fails it is not generally the tool or technology that was used, or the incompetence of the community manager (although those things can affect the communities growth and success), but it is more likely that you did not stick to the 3 R's.

- **Resources:** "Content is king!" without new and relevant content and conversations (or other types of interactions) there is no real reason for anyone to be there. Having unique content, or content that is created by the community members from the bottom up, will help to provide "stickiness" and keep the members coming back.

- **Recruiting:** Getting members into the community can often be the biggest obstacle to community success. If the community is part of any of the critical business processes that can be identified with "collaborative leverage" and are daily processes and can also become part of the person's behavior then the community will thrive. However, it is not enough to just attract members; you have to attract the right members. This includes a variety of roles including: community initiator, community manager, a cadre of regular contributors, and subject matter experts.

  In general, communities are composed of a few contributors and a high percentage of what can be deemed as "lurkers," in other words, those who read and take from the community but do not write and contribute to the community. This balance is critical; in most communities, the ratio of contributors to lurkers is around 2% to 98%. If your community has between 5%-10% contributors, it is considered a very active and successful community. Some smaller communities (fewer than 100 people) have a contributor percentage in the 20-30% range, but these are mostly in corporate environments, and in these cases, sometimes compensation is tied to community participation.

- **Recognition:** One of the best ways to get people to contribute is to reward them. Different people respond to different rewards. Salespeople often respond best to monetary or material rewards, while programmers, scientists, and technical people often respond best to peer recognition or rewards of status or access to highly sought-after projects, information, or equipment. In one HP community, the manager used frequent flyer miles to help get the community started, rewarding contributions that were scored highly by other community members (so rating and ranking functions, as well as "reputation engines" are often a standard part of community software).

  One of the best ways to start to design and plan your community is to understand what the potential community participants want to get out of it. Although surveys and focus groups can be helpful, a much richer and more productive route to understanding potential community needs is to do ethnographic or "day-in-the-life" studies of each of the roles or populations in the community. From these studies, a "user story" can be created for each group that will use the community.

A good example of this is some of the pro bono work I am doing with the Sophia's Garden Foundation (SGF) in creating HICO (Healing in Community Online), a project for which I have been privileged to be an advisor for the last year. My initial work with SGF was to have them create user stories for each of the roles in the community: the parent of the terminally sick child, the sick child, friends, and other family related to the sick child, medical practitioners dealing with the sick child, etc. Once these were created, we started looking at developing rapid prototypes of the community to start to get feedback from each of the target groups in the community (which we built in Qwaq).

It has been said that "it is hard to change what you can't measure." This is true in communities and social networks also. It is important to understand what the goals of the community are and to have some metrics that help you determine if the community is reaching those goals. A launch strategy is also critical in getting the community started. What I am saying is that thought, planning, research, and design of the community before you even consider what technologies or tools to use is a best practice.

Often we have been called in to deal with communities that focused on the technology first, and never really got off the ground. The technology is just an enabler of the person-to-person interactions, which are the critical piece. I keep telling the Sophia's Garden people, "Don't get so entranced with the technologies that you forget the people; community is about people first and foremost."

Power to the People!

The second part of this book (mostly written by Stewart) focuses on people. How people interact and communicate with each other, and especially how they do this as virtual teams or in geographically distributed, multi-organizational, and multi-cultural environments. The goal is to provide not only an overview of collaboration technologies and business processes that have "collaborative leverage" but to also look at best practices for people in these environments.

Part II
Collaboration: Process and People

In Part I, David said that:

> Collaboration 2.0 includes all of the outcomes, benefits and values of Collaboration 1.0—but takes place in a virtual world, or in cyberspace via the computer. It requires an evolutionary leap in relationship building with others in a global, networked, cross border, cross industry, cross department, cross-functional environment.
>
> Necessity is the mother of invention. As we moved to a knowledge-based economy with multi-national organizations, it became an imperative to work closely with others we may never meet face to face. That fact of organizational life has driven us to the new frontiers of Collaboration 2.0. The challenge many have taken up is that of: *developing the same capacity, creativity, and competence to work efficiently and effectively with our virtual colleagues across the boundaries of time, space, culture and the same complex challenges inherent in working with other human beings in the ever-changing external and internal landscape.*

No matter how sophisticated, technology is a conduit through which people send and receive messages. Beneath the gadgets and software are the words, processes, tools, and techniques that build a bridge of shared meaning between two or more people. Technology is not a substitute for the power of creativity and productivity that surfaces when a group of people is synchronized in pursuit of a clear shared vision. Technology can facilitate an exquisite exchange, and elegantly enable collaboration over long distances. When used intelligently, technology can contribute to a more effective world than the one that is currently inhabited. The purpose of this part of the book is to create communication awareness and learn "bridge-building" tools; including how to both prevent and quickly resolve disagreements. It is designed to impact how you think about communication, collaboration, and conflict resolution.

8 Critical Aspects of Human Interpersonal Communication

"The man who gets the most satisfactory results is not always the man with the most brilliant single mind, but rather the man who can best co-ordinate the brains and talents of his associates."—W. Alton Jones

Delivering Messages in a Collaboration 2.0 Environment

Communicating with other human beings can be a challenging, difficult activity: The more challenging the potential roadblocks (like distance, culture, and style differences), the greater the degree of difficulty. Some people think there is a class of people lucky enough to be born with great communication skills, while the rest are mortals who slog their way through the activity of human communication. That is far from the truth. Communicating is hard work, but most people who want to, can become good communicators. Just as people become experts in technical areas—programming, accounting, and technical writing—people can become experts in the art of communication. It's a matter of understanding the territory, and mastering the skills, moves, and tools. Figure 27 illustrates just how complex communicating a message really is—there are many structural challenges and potential roadblocks in the territory even when everyone has the best intention.

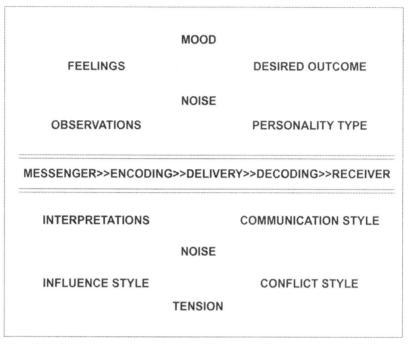

Figure 27: Communication Pathways

Aside from the differences in people, the external context magnifies the challenges as one moves faster and faster under a barrage of new information, in a constantly changing environment with new collaborators and shifting priorities without F2F contact.

What has been missing and what is a key ingredient for successful 2.0 collaboration are some tutorials and protocols around the basics of interpersonal communication. If people do not become students of understanding the nuances of how to communicate most effectively in a virtual environment, they will be forced to face the same consequences of ineffective communication as in the physical world. The opportunity is to create a context in which people communicate much more effectively, and that the skills used in the virtual world translate and carry over from cyberspace.

As will be demonstrated, good communicators know the message they want received, the audience who will be listening, the roadblocks they will have to go through, and the other variables at play. In a 2.0 setting, among other things, they have to communicate the nuance of tone, mood, emotion, and urgency by using words like literary prose or their "emoticon" equivalents.

Receiving Messages in a Collaboration 2.0 Environment

Listening is the most critical skill in communication. Paying attention is what builds relationship and connection. Listening is not a passive skill. Listening is about actively engaging with what is being said, as well as the context and the sender. It's about understanding your own bias and factoring that into your interpretation of the words said. It's about paying attention to the nuance and medium through which the message is delivered.

All that is true in a 1.0 environment may not necessarily carry over to the virtual world. Yet, some of the same assessments must be made to accurately interpret the messages that one receives in a 2.0 environment.

Building Bridges in a Collaboration 2.0 Environment

The art of communication is building bridges that create shared meaning. When individuals are together physically a smile, a touch, a look, a nod, locked eyes; all signify a moment of connection, shared meaning, and understanding. That immediate feedback loop provides immediate information about the effectiveness of the transmission. Those kinds of vehicles are not yet part of a 2.0 environment. That holds both good and bad news. The bad news is that a different set of tools, a different mindfulness, and nuanced assessments must be present—and that takes an additional level of attention.

The good news is that in a 1.0 arena all the above senses of connection can be deceiving. Sometimes the implicit understanding of a smile, a touch, a look, a nod, or locked eyes are not accurate because both the sender and receiver have different implicit understandings. In a 2.0 environment, the higher demand for verbal explicitness, although it requires more work, eliminates a great deal of the misunderstanding that comes from implicit connection. On the flip side, the sense of immediate feedback and feeling is more challenging to discern, though no less important.

What's Possible?

Steve Piersanti, the president of Berrett-Koehler, a well-known publishing company, understood that the success of a mission-driven publisher depended on an engaged group of authors that could bring a community to life, and in doing so would better serve the organizational mission. With that aim in mind, the following accomplishments have been generated out of a virtual community using very rudimentary technology:

- Seven author's retreats with 35-45 authors attending.

- Two marketing workshops with almost 50 people attending.

- One large scale community event with almost 400 in attendance.

- The birth of an independent Authors Cooperative with 75 members and an emerging web presence through which the work of the cooperative will be accomplished.

There can be no doubt that what made this possible was that many of the author participants were organizational consultants. They had a keen sense of self-awareness and well developed interpersonal skills. They had built into their personal operating systems many of the tools and protocols that will be suggested over the next few chapters. For some, all that follows will be validation of what they already know. For many who have been focused elsewhere, it will open a new world of awareness and understanding.

Creating Engagement, Shared Meaning and Context

The first step in creating engagement is finding common space in terms of a place for collaboration. Flip charts, white boards, yellow pads, and the like are that common space. Technology easily provides analogs. The next step is finding common ground in terms of a desired outcome for the collaboration. To create that engagement, shared meaning, and context it is important to establish the value or benefit each person believes they will receive from the collaboration. If they do not believe the value is adequate, they will not be inspired to engage with others. The negative motivation is the consequence of failing to correct something when "fixing" is the goal. Making the carrot and stick explicit will go a long way in creating the context of engagement and shared meaning.

Table 3: Communication Roadblocks

1. Lack of Clear Agreements
2. Personality Style Differences
3. Different Observations/Perceptions
4. Different Interpretations/Language
5. Different Feelings
6. Different Needs/Outcomes
7. Different Cultures
8. Different Genders
9. Urgency
10. Stakes

The best communicators see and anticipate the roadblocks to building shared vision. What sets them apart is their ability to scan the territory, recognize, anticipate, understand, strategize, and choose the mode, tone and words of the communication with a specific end in mind. When one option does not work they keep taking different routes until they build a bridge and a shared meaning emerges.

Their attitude: I will discover the path and make the connection.

Here are some common communication roadblocks and the way through them:

1. **Lack of Clear Agreements:** Usually this comes about because people did not take the time to make their agreements explicit and they have different implicit understandings of what they are doing together. The mistake that is most often made in these situations is stepping into the "Who Moved My Cheese" mindset of looking for who's at fault so that the buck can be passed. The quick solution, put a new agreement in place, or create one if none exists.

2. **Personality Style Differences:** The archetypes noted psychologist Carl Jung developed explanation for a great many of the communication challenges that come up when trying to communicate with other people. Instead of attributing communication difficulties to bad intention or lack of skills, the challenges are easily explained by inherent style differences.

   These style differences include:

   a. **Relating to the world:** Introverts relate more to their own inner life than extroverts who readily engage with others.

   b. **Dealing with details:** Precise people focus on the details of what's going on around them while unstructured people focus on the bigger picture and have little time for details.

   c. **Pace:** People who are urgent have a sense that things must be done immediately while deliberate people move along at a steady pace.

   d. **Getting your way:** Direct people ask for what they want while indirect people are much more nuanced and diplomatic in asking for what they want.

   These are a few of the common personality style differences. When you are at opposite ends of the spectrum, you tend to miss the content of the words spoken because you see things in a different way and react from a different perspective and emotional ground. The best practice when you know the receiver is a stylistic opposite is to assess them and design your message with what their style in mind. It is critical to remember that most communication breakdowns result from what can be deemed "structural factors." They result from legitimate differences that are revealed because of the many vectors that come into play when an individual does their best to communicate effectively.

3. **Different Observations/Perceptions:** Three people looking at the same scene or occurrence can see different things. The TRUTH is often elusive. Each individual has their own definition of truth in any given situation. It is best to accept differences in perceptual systems as part of the structure of human communication.

4. **Different Interpretations/Language:** "How long is a short meeting?" As a writer, lawyer, and communicator, I will be quick to point out there are many pitfalls, shortfalls, and pratfalls lurking in language. It is wise to always think about how someone else might interpret the particular words you choose.

5. **Different Feelings:** Your feeling reaction to a particular situation is a reflection of the sum of your life experiences up until that moment in time. People with different experiences will have a different feeling reaction when something does or does not happen. Someone who had an abusive father might be not be very happy about having a new female boss while someone who had a close warm relationship with their dad might be very pleased by the same change? It is critical to pay attention to the different feeling states generated by others out of their unique experience. It is critical to get to know them, honor them, and act accordingly.

6. **Different Needs / Outcomes:**

   Some want fame

   Some want money

   Some want promotions

   Some want responsibility

   Some want recognition

   Some want to be better than _____

Sometimes we don't think about them. Most are content to operate under the wonderful "Golden Rule"– *Do unto others as you would have them do unto you.* That's good, that's honorable, and that's giving. Unfortunately, that is self referential. It assumes "they" operate out of the same standard as you and hold dear what you hold dear. "The Platinum Rule" is much more effective.

Do unto others as they would do unto themselves.

When you want to motivate or satisfy someone, it is much more effective to reward and motivate them by offering what THEY want.

7. **Different Cultures:** While working under U.S. norms, people often deal with folks from all over the globe on a regular basis so it's critical to pay attention to the nuance, stylistic, and normative differences. It is also important to remember that most individuals are more alike than different.

8. **Different Genders:** We do have different styles of communication. That's why the author John Grey had a best seller with "Men are from Mars, Women are from Venus."[25] Women tend to be more indirect than men. While a woman may state that there is nothing bothering her, most men who have been married for enough years to know better, will realize that her statement is nothing more than an introduction to a plethora of issues that are soon to come to fruition. Whereas a man will be more than happy to walk through the door yelling and screaming about all of his problems, including some that may not even be his own.

9. **Urgency:** Most are operating on a sped up sense of time. Although "everything" is urgent, there are some who move along deliberately. It's critical to understand the sense of time others have or risk definitely "missing" each other as we operate in different time zones. It is also essential to have specific dates when talking about tasks.

10. **Stakes:** In most all situations there are different potential consequences for different people. You should always be aware of what's at stake for others. How mission critical is the project or your promised performance. How do they need to be treated? Get on the same train in terms of speed, time, and destination.

---

25. John Grey, *Men are from Mars, Women are from Venus,* (New York: Harper Collins, 1992).

The Conflict Continuum

When approaching the realm of conflict you can look through many lenses. The following continuum provides a good sequential overview of the process of addressing conflict.

Table 4:   The Conflict Continuum

1. Stress	2. Managing Emotion	3. Collaborative Negotiation
Body sensations deliver the message	Everyone acknowledges the conflict	Negotiation begins
Often the other person does not acknowledge a conflict exists	Emotional static is reduced so that productive negotiation can begin	The conflict is resolved

1. **Signs of Conflict:** The first sign that something needs attention is the "disease" of stress. Feeling stress is the result of the flight/fright part of humanity's pre-historic lizard brain. Many thousands of years ago humans ignored that discomfort at their peril. Lunch is what became of them if they did not heed the warning. To this day many ignore the discomfort at their own peril. When stress is sensed, it is a clear sign that something is going on that needs to be addressed. Unfortunately, many of us make the mistake of not paying attention as they fool themselves into believing that the situation will take care of itself. It usually does not. If left alone, it will fester, the emotion will increase and the cost of not paying attention will increase. The good news is that although the feeling is uncomfortable, that discomfort is conveying a very important message: it is essential to ask yourself what needs attention and who needs to be communicated with, but first...

2. **Managing Emotion:** Conflict is resolved through some form of collaborative negotiating process. It is almost impossible to engage in that kind of conversation when an individual is emotionally triggered. The trigger often takes the form of either passive or aggressive behavior. When passive most will try to run away from the situation and when aggressive many run right through it. Neither is effective. More important, when you are in that agitated state, it is

essential to manage the emotion before engaging in some dialogue process. When emotionally triggered, more often than not, the dialogue will reflect the emotion that is being felt. What must be done is the emotion needs to be managed before engaging.

By the time adulthood is reached, most folks have developed some personal techniques for balance. There are many activities that will get you there. To name a few:

Yoga	Listening to Music	http://www.Heartmath.com
Exercise	Reading	Drive in the Country
Swimming	Being in Nature	Dancing
"Time Out"	Playing with Pets	Switching Activities
Playing with Kids	Walking	Playing a Musical Instrument
Running	Aerobics	Visualization/Changing State

After you have burned off the emotion of the situation, you can begin thinking about engaging. It is often smart, as a matter of modeling and preparing, to assume a martial arts or skiing pose—legs slightly bent and shoulder width apart—imagine roots coming out of the bottom of your feet holding you solidly and firmly, planted and anchored to the earth. Now you are centered and present, ready to fully and truthfully engage. To quote noted cultural anthropologist Dr. Angelis Arrien from "The Four Fold Way," the task is to:

- Show Up
- Pay Attention
- Tell YOUR Truth
- Do not be attached to the outcome [26]

---

26. Angelis Arrien, *The Four-Fold Way: Walking the Paths of the Warrior, Teacher, Healer, and Visionary,* (New York: HarperOne, 1993).

My paraphrase:

- Be Present
- Listen
- Do not think you have THE truth
- See what shows up, be willing to learn and be influenced by what you hear, and be ready to shift your position

3. **Collaborative Dialogue/Negotiation:** Now it's time for the real fun to begin: negotiation with the other side. Through the bargaining, you get to appreciate what's happening "over there" and you get to express your needs and get your concerns cared for at the expense of no one. When we think about "negotiating," the frame that usually comes up is adversarial. It's either them OR me so I need to prevent them from getting what they want. And yet, the most powerful and effective negotiators understand that finding out what "they" want and figuring out how to achieve that for everyone involved is the MOST powerful form of negotiation. It's not about them OR me. It's about them AND me.

   Unfortunately, all this will take some practice, and that will require some stumbles and toe stubbing. That said, if you can instill a critical awareness and a "beginner's mind," then you have gone a long way toward making yourself a CONSCIOUS COMMUNICATOR.

9 Building Blocks: The Interpersonal Communication Toolbox

"Show Up
Pay Attention
Tell Your Truth
Don't Be Attached to the Outcome"

—Angelis Arrien, Ph.D.

As stated earlier, becoming a good communicator is hard, detailed, analytical work. But it is the most important muscle you can develop for being more effective in both your personal and professional life. Coordinating the work of many, developing teamwork, and fostering collaboration are the work of effective leadership and management. It is a skill that can be learnt.

In terms of communication in a virtual environment, paying attention to the details and nuances is the essential work. The following key principles seem to be universal, applying in both the F2F and virtual worlds, though applying them virtually will take some thought and intention.

Table 5:   The Communication Toolbox

Moving Through Roadblocks
No Difficult People – Only Different People
Instruments Demonstrate Differences
Developing Emotional Intelligence
Responding and Reacting
Anger and Aggression
"I" statements
Know / Do / Feel
S O F T E N
Mirroring / Identifying
Don't Bark Back at Barking Dogs
Listening Skills
Object / Subject
Goal "Agreements for Results"
Non-Verbal
Automatic Writing
Providing Effective Feedback
Delegating Effectively

Moving Through Roadblocks

The context in which we communicate is filled with the potential for miscommunication. Let's say you want to get a message to your colleague in Germany (they are fluent English, but it is after all a second language) about a new person who will join your team on a very large consulting project. You both have known this person for many years and have your own perceptions of them. Although they have the reputation of being a "technical genius," they have some quirky personal characteristics.

When you are about to share your perceptions of this person, you begin by coding the message through your own filters, then you deliver the message. When they receive the message, they decode it through their perceptual filters. Add to this the use of asynchronous e-mail and you begin to understand that filters and the medium present natural roadblocks to creating shared meaning, the goal of effective communication. All of these vectors prove how artful communication is, and how difficulties are usually more structural than intentional (see Figure 27 at the beginning of Chapter 8).

The most effective communicators work at it. They have the ability and persistence to both anticipate and move through roadblocks until shared meaning is created.

No Difficult People – Only Different People

Many have the tendency to give up too quickly and abandon their goal of building the bridge to the other. The assessment is often made that the other will not or cannot understand the message one is trying to deliver because they are too difficult. The common belief is that a critical distinction is realizing the difference between "difficult behavior," and "being difficult." One is about character, the other about action. This can be deemed as being behavioral, and that the behavior can be improved through the learning and feedback that is given in the spirit of generating improved effectiveness and delivered without revealing personal judgments.

Instruments Demonstrate Differences

There are many different instruments that reveal style differences in different aspects of communication. They include:

- PSI–Personal Styles Inventory
- DISC–Personality Profile
- MBTI–Myers Briggs
- Influence Inventory
- Relationship Strategies
- Thomas Killian Conflict Style

These instruments serve a few very useful purposes. They make us aware of the different ways people receive and deliver information. That usually explains why many are challenged when communicating with particular individuals. This enables the individual to use what they learn about their audiences so that they can communicate more effectively. Using an instrument for a team or workgroup and making people aware of the styles of others is a very useful tool for developing effectiveness in communicating with particular individuals.

The instruments reveal preferences along a continuum of opposite styles. They shed light on why you may be having difficulty communicating with particular individuals. They provide information and strategies on the best way to communicate with people of opposite or similar styles. They deliver the message that tends to have preferences because of their own experience, how they developed, or how through genetic inclination they have the capacity to consciously choose how to "flex" their style so they can be more effective in dealing with people who have different preferences. "Flexing" is the way we develop our communication muscles!

Developing Emotional Intelligence

Traditionally, intelligence was measured in terms of IQ (intelligence quotient), which measures cognitive ability. Of course that is a valuable measure of capacity. But it's not the only critical factor. There are a number of different kinds of intelligence that have value in working with others. One of the most important ones for working with others is "Emotional Intelligence" because communication involves the nuances of human interaction. The five basic tenants of emotional intelligence as conceived by Daniel Goleman and expressed in his book, *Working with Emotional Intelligence*, popularized the field.

1. **Self-Awareness:** This is the foundational skill that enables one to separate self from behavior through observation and reflection. It enables you to make more discerning assessments about yourself and your verbal and non-verbal communication.

2. **Self-Regulation:** The ability to control what you do or say and how you react in the face of communication coming at you.

3. **Empathy:** Your ability to stand in their shoes and understand their perspective. The following quote sums up empathy and compassion:

   If you knew the secret history of those you would like to punish, you would see a sorrow and suffering enough to disarm all your hostility.

4. **Self-Motivation:** The ability to be proactive and not wait for things to come at you.

5. **Social Skills:** Your capacity for navigating in groups of people and recognizing the impacts of your words and deeds on others.[27]

Responding and Reacting

How you engage with others is a critical part of the communication process. Whether you respond or react goes a long way in determining the outcome of the interaction. Responding has a much greater chance of getting you what you want while reacting is likely to engender push-back.

Reaction: Reply or behavior prompted by external influences that stimulate thought or behavior. The behavior is usually automatic or immediate. The critical factor is remembering:

YOU CANNOT UNPUNCH SOMEONE!

Response: A reply or behavior stemming from internal knowledge based on values, ethics and standards that have been personally developed. The response is based on a choice after reflection about the specific outcome you want. Self-editing is the critical skill.

Anger and Aggression

Anger is the emotion engendered by an expectation of or unacceptable behavior on the part of others. Aggression is the behavior to which you are driven to by unpleasant negative emotions including anger. These

---

27. Daniel Goleman, *Working With Emotional Intelligence*, (New York: Bantam Doubleday Dell Publishing Group, 2002).

will always get in the way. It's not unusual to feel anger as a result of someone's words or actions. The skill is to manage what you do in response.

Passive / Aggressive / Assertive

One way of looking at what you do after someone communicates with you is to choose how you respond. The choice might be characterized by one of the following modes:

Table 6: Passive Aggressive Assertive

PASSIVE	ASSERTIVE	AGGRESSIVE
Failure to care for self	Courage	Violate other's rights
Violation of your rights	Connection	Failure to care for them
	Caring	

Assertive behavior respects everyone's needs!

The chart sums it up beautifully! Following it is guaranteed to improve your effectiveness.

"I" Statements

This is one of the most critical and most underutilized techniques for effective communication. One of the greatest mistakes made is to criticize the words or deeds of another by judging them. A classic example is

"You make me so angry when you are late."

That is a double whammy: Blaming them for your negative emotion and judging their behavior as "late." This type of communication is guaranteed to generate the push-back of a defensive response. A much more effective message would be:

"I was very angry when you arrived at 9 when you promised to be here at 8."

Let them assess their behavior and you will likely get an apology and a promise to do better. The formula is

"I was ***your emotion*** when you ***describe their behavior***."

Know / Do / Feel

One of the key failures of the communication process is the failure to think carefully of the message you want to deliver before composing and delivering your words. This kind of communicating can be best described as "thinking out loud." It is the antithesis of the way the prolific Ernest Hemingway described his process: "I think a lot and write very little." For me, a simple formula for avoiding this pitfall is the mantra of:

"KNOW / DO / FEEL"

Before you deliver any communication it is imperative to ask yourself

"What do you want them to know?"
"How do you want them to feel?"
"What do you want them to do?"

If you do not have a clear answer to at least one of the questions, then you have nothing to say and you might refrain from speaking.

S O F T E N

This is a very useful acronym for real-time, F2F communication. Although the commands for that kind of communication are not exactly the same, they have great value for any kind of exchange. As related to the world of virtual communication:

Smile	Be pleasant in what you have to say. Communicate with diplomacy and tact even when delivering bad news. Be mindful of word choice.
Open	Do not hold back. Share the feelings behind your words when appropriate. Be available for the response.
Forward Lean	Engage with them, show you are interested.

Territory	Be aware by the response of when you have pushed too hard.
Eye Contact	Meet them and engage. Five to seven seconds.
Nod	Always acknowledge what they say to show you are listening.

Mirroring / Identifying

Communicating is about building a bridge between you and the other. It is always a give and take process. A critical act is the need to establish rapport before delivering your message. One of the best techniques for doing that is to mirror and identify. You want to send a message back with a similar mood or tone to establish connection. You can demonstrate your connection by showing that you understand what they are saying and by using an example from your own life. Once you are synchronized, you can deliver your message.

This technique takes a page from neuro-linguistic programming (NLP). This powerful body of communication tools from the 1980's was so popular in the world of sales and influencing others that some people were concerned it was unethical because of the inherent power of manipulation. The premise was that once you mirrored and established rapport you could then lead the conversation where you wanted it to go and others would follow at an unconscious level. Essentially, it puts people at ease which fosters open communication.

Don't Bark Back at Barking Dogs

The worst mistake you can make with people who are speaking louder to make their point is to try and "out louder" them. All that does is add fuel to the fire and generates an even louder response. When they are gripped in this kind of emotion, the best thing to do to de-escalate a situation is to speak about the facts that have made them so emotional. This return to reason will usually calm people down.

Listening Skills

Effective communication is a two-way, give and take, interactive, iterative process. It is essential to spend as much time hearing their message as composing yours. The best way to fully understand and appreciate the value of listening is to spend some time only listening. It may even help to wear sign suggesting:

"I'm not speaking today, only listening."

before moving through your ordinary day. You would be amazed at how much you miss because you are focused on your own voice and what you will say in response to what you hear, never fully giving yourself to the listening process because you are already focused on responding before they have finished, and before you have fully digested the message. Here are some tips that will help:

1. **Active Listening:** This means whole being listening. Realizing what is behind the words, observing with your eyes, ears and heart and thinking about what is not being said. It requires using your thinking speed wisely to interpret and fill in the blank spaces that their words do not fill because your mind is much quicker processing information than their ability to speak.

2. **Paraphrasing:** This is the best way to make sure the bridge is connected – feed the message back in your words and see if you are connected by the shared meaning that is established.

3. **Engage Fully:** Give them all of your ATTENTION and PRESENCE.

4. **Environment/Distractions:** Make sure nothing gets in the way of you and them. Sorry, multi-tasking may be great in theory but when your attention is diluted you miss critical parts of the message and you distance the speaker.

5. **Do Not Interrupt:** One of our biggest mistakes is cutting people off after they deliver part of their message. We begin asking a question based on what we think is important and their message gets completely lost.

6. **Hold Judgments:** Human minds function like judgment machines making relative comparisons about what is seen, heard, and thought...

   Hair is too long
   Poor choice of words
   That will never work
   Terrible idea

   ...

   It is best to observe your judgments, hold them in abeyance, and not think you have the truth and must act upon what crosses your mind at a point in time. That way you can listen all the way through and make a more considered response.

7. **Ask questions:** This demonstrates you are interested and provides a more complete explication and understanding of what is said.

8. **Take notes:** Rather than interrupt save your questions by taking notes

9. **Do not anticipate** what they are saying or focus on your response: Wait until they are done, digest and then respond to the message.

10. **The Best Tool**

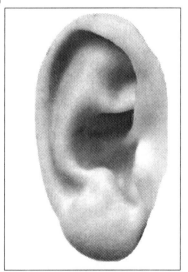

Figure 28: The Most Powerful Communication Tool

Figure 29: Listening Role Model

Figure 30: Elements of Communication

Object / Subject

Martin Buber makes the very important distinction of

"I / It" and "I / Thou"

relationships. I / "It" relationships are object oriented—many think of others as objects to be used and manipulated for their own purposes. I / "Thou" relationships are subjective—you care about the person.[28]

One of the tragedy's of the global corporate culture is that it has reduced others to objects; instruments for one's own advancement. People become tools to use to accomplish this or that and those who do the using often suffer the lack of not knowing them as individuals. If one can step beyond that cultural tendency and relate to others as compassionate human beings then the connections and communications will be far more effective. The "I / Thou" context will generate a much deeper level of concern and respect and they will listen more attentively to your messages.

Goal "Agreements for Results"

The best and most effective communication has a purpose in mind—action. Otherwise, talk is mere banter. What can we agree TO DO together? The goal is joint action. Everything else is often frustrating idle chit-chat. The purpose of collaborative communication is to construct a shared vision in terms of desired accomplishment and a road-map to it. You can think in terms of an "arranged marriage" with no divorce when it comes to working with virtual teammates. You can spend your life in agonizing rebellion, or you can chose to love it.

---

28. Martin Buber, *I and Thou* (New York: Free Press, 1971).

Non-Verbal

Communication is composed of three parts:

Visual – Appearance of the Deliverer

Vocal – Tone or Mood of our Message

Verbal – Content of the Words

About ninety percent of what is "said" is non-verbal. Individuals communicate by the way they look and the tone, mood, and affect of what they say. This is critical to remember. You can deliver any kind of news and minimize the "push-back" depending on your appearance and the tone of your message. This takes on a huge amount of importance when delivering bad news electronically. It is essential to use words or other symbolic visual and tonality representations when dealing in a verbal medium. The art of narrative becomes a critical skill as you do your best to add visual and tonal components to verbal communication.

Automatic Writing

When you are triggered with emotion and want to dash off a letter of rage please do compose it and just let the rage ramble through the page. Do not send it. ALWAYS ADDRESS IT TO YOURSELF OR PUT IT IN A WORD FILE. Come back in twenty-four hours and think about the RESPONSE you really want to send in terms of the end result you are looking for. You can also use this technique if you are unsure of HOW you want to respond. Write for ten minutes to discover the response inside you.

Providing Effective Feedback

When you are providing feedback you are usually responding to another person's product or service or opinions. In doing so, especially when it's negative feedback, take care of the person and provide actionable information. The tips for doing it well include:

- Comment on the behavior, not the person
- Timeliness is essential
- For negative feedback consider telephone as a better channel

- Remember you're in a long term relationship
- Be constructive, not judgmental—tell them what they can do and by when
- Be specific
- Ask if it would be valuable for them
- Remember, it's about growth and learning

Delegating Effectively

When giving someone something to do, it is critical to provide clear directions that are:

- Specific
- Measurable
- Have a "by when"
- Part of an ongoing conversation
- Negotiable

10 Developing "Resolutionary" Thinking

"Imagination is more important than knowledge."
—Albert Einstein

In difficult situations, your manner of communication is the critical ingredient for producing the kind of response and results you want. And, sometimes the best actions are counter-intuitive to what dominant cultural values might suggest.

There are two mantras that may have value when communicating in the virtual world:

Some people never learn...

Smart people learn from their own mistakes...

Geniuses can learn from the mistakes of others!

****

Some people do not know what to do in challenging situations

Smart people know what to do in difficult situations

Geniuses know how to think about challenging situations

Working in the virtual world is inherently a challenging situation because it requires compensating for missing paths over which the majority have assumed information and metadata was transmitted. Communicating effectively in the virtual world demands becoming a

"Conscious Communicator"

For many years, Max DePree was the CEO of the Herman Miller Company. During that time, the Herman Miller Company was consistently named one of the best companies to work for in the US. When asked why they were so successful and why people liked working for them, he said he believed it was because of the relationships, which he deemed to be the fabric of the company. Max said that all relationships—internal, external, with suppliers, customers and among departments—were based on "COVENANT."[29] In translation—relationships were both a meeting of the mind and heart. It is interesting to compare this to the standard for creating a legal relationship which is based on a "meeting of the mind" only. Covenant is the kind of bedrock connection on which resolutionary thinking is premised. The ongoing aspiration is for all relationships to be moving toward to the state of covenant: a meeting of mind and heart, a sense of agreement and resolution.

The Attitude of Resolution

Creating, sustaining, and renewing agreements is critical because good agreements create the shared vision and culture, and prevent conflict in all kinds of collaborations. Cultivating an attitude of resolution will reveal wisdom, resources, and practical tools for taking that attitude into all aspects of life, with the arena of Collaboration 2.0 being a great place to learn and experiment.

---

29. Max DePree, *Leadership In as Art* (New York: Bantam Doubleday Dell Publishing Group, 1989).

What is Culture?

Is there a simple and elegant way of building and transforming an organizations' culture? The phrase "cultural change" triggers the question when repeatedly stated as a goal for organizational strategic initiatives. It may be accurate to say that a cultural change is what is required to operate in a virtual world. *So, what does this mean?*

An organization's culture includes social and behavioral actions and experiences, such as:

- The way work is organized and experienced

- How authority is exercised and distributed

- How people are and feel rewarded, organized, and controlled

- The values and work orientation of the staff

- The degree of formalization, standardization, and control through systems

- The value placed on planning, analysis, logic, and fairness

- How much initiative, risk-taking, scope for individuality and expression is given

- Rules and expectations about such things as formality in interpersonal relations, dress, and personal eccentricity

- Importance of rules, procedures, specifications of performance and results, for a team or an individual

Different organizations have different cultures. For example:

- Autocratic, benevolent autocratic, consultative, and participative

- Mechanistic and organic

- Simple structure, machine bureaucracy, divisionalized, professional bureaucracy, and adhocracy

- Power, role, task, and personal

- Learning organization

- Pushy, harsh, and authoritarian

- Political

- Rule and ritual bound

- Cold and separated

- Brisk, dynamic, opportunistic

- Exploitative, no give, and all take

- Caring and genuinely interested in people as people

Organizational culture may be visible in the type of buildings, offices, and shops of the organization, or in the image projected in public relations. Think for example of the differences between a local authority, a computer manufacturer, and a merchant bank. An organization's culture may be imperceptible, taken for granted, assumed—a status quo that many individuals participate and live in but do not question. Elements of the culture may be questioned where individual or group expectations do not correspond to the behaviors associated with the prevailing values of those who uphold "the culture." An organization may display elements of several "cultures" which may contradict each other, or compete. The characteristics of an anti-organizational or countervailing culture can even be considered.

To understand an organization's cultures you can begin by describing the type of organization from the examples above. The descriptions are representative "models." The model defines elements of engagement and relationships. Models enable the prediction of events so that one's own behavior can be influenced along with the behavior of others.

Creating Culture

"Culture" is a "fuzzy" word. A more focused, and universal understanding would be useful. Culture reflects the quality and character of organizational relationships. In fact and effect, the nature of all organizational relationships, both internal and external, reflect and embody the culture. The sum of relationships is culture. The quality and character of organizational relationships reflect the nature and quality of the web of implicit and explicit agreements that are the foundation and glue of organizational relationships.

Regardless of how you might categorize or develop a particular culture one key to satisfaction, success, accomplishment, and productivity is the ability to effectively cultivate and sustain sequential and concurrent long term relationships. In fact, this is true both personally, and at work. Organizational effectiveness in business, government, non-profit or educational organizations depends on the quality of relationships. Without high quality relationships an organization will be challenged in its ability to accomplish its mission or even to survive. Examples of these key relationships include:

- Raising capital
- Building teams
- Opening and closing sales
- Fostering long-term employment relationships
- Developing new products
- Developing leadership succession plans

The quality of organizational relationships depends on the quality of the agreements among and between every person in the organization. This is true for agreements between: individuals and the organization, the organization with its stakeholders, between departments, among team members, and with reporting relationships. This is certainly true in the face-to-face world, and it becomes even more fundamental in the virtual world.

Unfortunately, most people never develop a specific kind of conversational competence that enables them to establish and sustain effective long term collaborative relationships. Most of us never learn how to think and what to talk about in building solid agreements with team members; direct reports; supervisors; suppliers; and all members of a virtual team. They never learn how to deal with conflict in a non-adversarial way, or how to create ground rules for moving through challenging times. But through experience, everyone understands the huge payoff of being able to engage in dialogues that both create and sustain long-term relationships which lead to high levels of performance and effective, happy people.

These collaborative understandings are best designated as:

"Agreements for Results"

Rather than thinking about how you might protect yourself or get an edge, the conversational template in Chapter 13 enables people to create and sustain effective relationships, and contributes to a culture of high performance. Before getting to the conversational templates that guide the creation of Agreements for Results, it is important to explore the thinking that is fundamental to it.

Principles of Resolutionary Thinking

Table 7: Principles of Resolutionary Thinking[30]

1. Abundance
2. Efficiently Creating and Sustaining Collaborations
3. Creativity
4. Fostering Resolution
5. Becoming Open
6. Long-Term Collaborations
7. Honoring Logic, Feelings & Intuition
8. Disclosing Information & Feelings
9. Learning
10. Becoming Response Able

The following sections elaborate on these principles.

---

30. Stewart Levine, *Getting to Resolution* (San Francisco: Berrett-Koehler, 1998).

1. Abundance

Abundance is a part of and is the foundation for all principles. If you don't believe there is "enough"—enough for you to get what you want AND for others to get what they want reaching an agreement will be very challenging because your starting positions will be as adversaries. If you believe there is enough, following the other nine principles will enable powerful collaborations. It will not always be easy, but it can be simple. Abundance, among other things, means knowing there is a collaboration to be discovered that will satisfy everyone.

Abundance is the keystone of Resolutionary Thinking. There is no limit to what creativity can produce. The same principles of unlimited creativity can be applied to problem solving and conflict resolution.

All profit, value, wealth, and accumulation result from combining the energy and talent of a group of people. Think of a new business, a new team, or a community project that you were once a part of. The value of the business, the contribution to the larger organization, or the benefit to the community came from someplace. Microsoft started as an idea in someone's mind. The creative energy of many people coming together and the innovations they have designed have made many millionaires, and a few billionaires. The source came from an unlimited supply of abundant potential. Before Microsoft, the whole domain of PCs as personal productivity tools barely existed.

It's your choice. If you choose the principle of abundance when you come together to create a new agreement or to resolve a conflict about an existing agreement, you can step into a field of enormous potential. It's not you OR me; it's not us OR them—it's you AND me, us AND them. No matter the situation, you can have what you want if you tap into the abundant supply of creativity available to everyone.

2. Efficiently Creating and Sustaining Collaborations

Most habits waste enormous amounts of resources for resolving conflict and reaching agreement. A key principle in resolutionary thinking is to conserve human and material resources by making the agreement and resolution process efficient by following a specific conversational road-map. If an efficient process for establishing front-end agreements and a resolution processes are established at the beginning of a project, they will enable a team to stay focused on productivity and goals. Although you never know what will happen on a journey, it is better not to begin unless you can maximize your chances for success.

Creating Agreements Efficiently

Unfortunately "winning" and the adversarial mind-set pervades our thinking in many collaborative situations. Many overlook the value of doing their best to make sure the partnership or team will be effective. The process of putting an effective agreement in place on the front end requires addressing many specific aspects of what you will do together, including acknowledging that conflict, and mapping out a strategy for dealing with it. Conflict prevention in action is present when you agree on how you will agree, and how you will disagree, inevitable aspects of a functional collaborative relationship.

Creating an Efficient Collaboration

Getting a successful project up and running is an exercise in forming a collaborative team. That requires going through some conflict, but not as much as traditional experience would have you expect. Traditional thinking says that teams go through the stages of: forming, storming, norming, and performing. All conflict involved in passing through these stages may not be avoided, but it can be minimized when:

1. A team agreement is put in place at the beginning, and

2. Everyone is willing to use the Resolutionary principles and models to quickly engage in conversations for resolution when conflict arises.

The primary challenge is learning to quickly identify and let go of the fear that your needs will not be taken care of or that they will be compromised. The key learning is embracing a mind-set of abundance—realizing everyone can win without the need for a loser. Keeping your eyes on the big picture, seeing the forest through the trees and losing certain battles for the sake of the war are clichés, but they emphasize that continuing is usually more efficient than leaving, despite the temporary conflict. Starting over and/or arguing is pure inefficiency.

People who are working together often waste resources because they do not have a clearly articulated vision of where they are going and how they will get there. They waste more resources resolving the inevitable conflicts that surface because they have not done the work at the beginning. The difference is clearly understood as the difference between

"Ready – Fire – Aim!"

and

"Ready – Aim – Fire!"

3. Creativity

Most people are conditioned to think in terms of issues and problems. Experts try to fix problems in a way that satisfies their professional standards of what is right. A belief system has been instilled within most folks that states: conflict and disagreement are bad, which causes the masses to get emotionally upset when confronted with conflict and differences. There seems to be a prevailing attitude that all things should be perfect, smooth, and without rough edges. Should they not? Aren't you entitled to be upset when they aren't?

When you add "problem thinking" to "conflict is bad" and throw in the fear of consequences of conflict, the chance of getting trapped multiplies. Moving to a more abundant, unlimited field of creativity enhances the potential for satisfactory resolution because it removes the constraints and broadens the field of potential solutions.

In fact, many people would be better off if they saw the clash of differences as an ordinary and expected part of working with others. Most people are without a doubt going to address the problems and issues that upset, concern, or worry them. Many people have difficulty accepting that life is filled with surprises, conflict, disappointment, and unmet expectations. These things happen—consistently and predictably.

Self-reflection is a key part of living in the principle of creativity. Programming one's self not to use the word *problem* when facing any potential conflict situation is very useful. Framing the situation as an "opportunity to demonstrate your creativity" is a far more productive approach. Before your emotions render you useless, step into observer/listener and think about what would be the most effective action. When someone tells you he or she has a problem to deal with just smile and say, "We have an opportunity to demonstrate how creative we can be." The key is how you talk to yourself. By stating "the situation is an opportunity and not a problem," it allows you to be far more resourceful.

4. Fostering Resolution

The fire of conflict can be fanned by following practices that have become hard wired by poor role models and even poorer procedures. In the Resolutionary Thinking paradigm it is critical to ask "what will quickly enable me to move through the conflict and get to a resolution without making things worse?"

In the Resolutionary Thinking paradigm, reaching agreements and addressing differences take place within a context of collaboration. Creative, collaborative systems for making agreements and resolving conflicts are the norm. Reaching agreement is no longer an adversarial negotiation. Instead of negotiating you are having a dialogue about creating a composite, shared vision of the desired outcome. Built into the agreement is the understanding that disagreement will happen. Everyone is developing a healthy relationship with conflict because they are no longer triggered by it.

Traditional conversational models for resolving differences can be like spraying gasoline on fire. The flames get hotter and higher. Although there are situations in which anger is appropriate it is much healthier for people to learn to deal with their own emotion and come to a dialogue ready to look for solutions. Dealing with disagreements is an opportunity to deepen the agreement, and should not be viewed as a breakdown. All are inside the same circle, standing together, shoulder to shoulder, wondering how best to take care of their shared concerns while envisioning together the future and results they want to create.

5. Becoming Open

Posturing and righteous bravado do not help reaching an agreement. They keep you distant and prevent concerns from being addressed. Many have been programmed by cultural role models and need to unlearn and adopt a better way through practice and the experience of the power and simplicity of being open and present. Often, people in conflict posture, they play games. Their focus is more about being right than being effective. In many contexts being right and winning has become important. Unfortunately, no one gets points for candor.

Being open is an easy, natural way to be—it is not being weak. It takes great strength to refrain from being reactionary in a situation. Being open is being your real, authentic self. Getting beyond your initial resistance is challenging. But once beyond that resistance, it is the easiest behavior to adopt. People often become engulfed in bravado because they have never seen another option. There are few visible role models for this behavior. Many would be surprised that the qualities that most people find admirable are: honesty, listening, authenticity, lack of ego, and understanding another perspective.

Being open is best summed up by Dr. Arrien who has written the four guides for all human interaction. You are fully present, without an act, story, or angle. You tell YOUR truth without the belief that it is "THE" truth. You do not need to have the outcome be a certain way—you are available to discover a way that serves everyone better than what you had thought. That is a great way to stay centered and empty emotional attachment that can only lead to trouble. There is no acting or scheming; you are simply yourself. It's easy because you don't worry about being consistent with your previous "act" or story; you don't have to second-guess yourself or posture. You just show up and tell YOUR truth and LISTEN to the truths of others.

6. Long-Term Collaborations

Most companies are conditioned to think in terms of a short-term horizon—an immediate victory. They see only this quarter's bottom line. You can choose to operate from a short-term or a long-term perspective. If you think and act as if the collaboration will be long term, you will feel much better about the relationship and yourself. You never know when the relationship will take on long-term significance, or when you will have to face the other person in your neighborhood. How many stories have your heard about someone being interviewed for a position by someone who once reported to them?

Fear is often the driver, and that can make any situation adversarial. Fear precludes trust and generates adversaries you want to control. They are the enemy. Sadly, fear often unconsciously operates between people who want to collaborate. Society has been influenced by an era of "Lone-Rangerism"—solo-riding, conquer-the-west, rugged-individual, Marlboro-man, immediate-gratification, this-quarter, "me" generation! The dissonant imperative of teams, collaboration, and virtual organizations are creating havoc in many people's minds.

Vast changes must be made in the way people view others. Personal programming is driving society to be top-gun, king-of-the-hill, victorious individuals—now. The patience it takes to work with others is what is really needed, but it's not the way the majority has been conditioned. This paradox stems from these two contradictory messages:

Competition vs. Cooperation

"Winning" has been deeply embedded as the prominent mindset of the global business community. The word win is synonymous with success. Unfortunately, it also implies the corresponding "losing." Even though the term win-win is used in many places, most people think "for me to win, you must lose." Though win-win speak has been pervasive in organizations, the idea of everyone winning is not yet an operational principle people fully embrace because they don't know how to make it happen. Though the words are spoken, the people do not believe or fully understand them. This is a great source of inner conflict, and the confusion pulls people in opposite directions. Working in the virtual world provides a great opportunity to shift the paradigm and create a new way of working.

7. Honoring Logic, Feelings & Intuition

Although attitudes are shifting most people still believe that the world operates on the premise of logic. Aristotle and Newton would be proud of how their basic cognitive precepts are being followed about how the world works. Everything fits into a category, A flows from B, and consequences are predictable.

Beyond the Five Senses

We are on the verge of stepping onto a new foundation. There are many challenges whose solutions are so complex that new theoretical models are needed for the solutions and resolutions. Albert Einstein predicted that new models of thinking would be needed to solve the situations he saw on the horizon.

In domains previously thought to be grounded only in the world of logic, there is now a broader spectrum of "human-beingness." Feelings and intuition are standing along side logic. This applies to collaborating in two important ways:

1. The reliance on logic, feelings, AND intuition in creating effective collaborations

2. The usage of logic, feelings, AND intuition as a factor in determining that an agreement has been reached.

When dealing with people, you must factor in emotions because they are present in all situations. In more and more arenas, the nonlinear and sometimes the non-rational are accepted. Trust is much more important than a tightly drafted contract. The "phenomenon" of a covenantal agreement is the heartfelt assessment of agreement after engaging in the "process" of discussing essential elements that make up their collaboration. You can say all the right words; it can look tidy, and still not be an agreement because something is missing at a gut level. There is no covenant. There is no meeting of mind and heart.

8. Disclosing Information & Feelings

Information is the critical lifeblood of an organization. For some, cutting off communication is an accepted way of participation. Nondisclosure dilutes the ability to reach agreement. Information is the raw material that leads to agreement. Holding information can only lead to mistrust and escalation of conflict. Full disclosure is evidence of a good faith effort to work together.

When disagreement erupts, often the flow of information halts. People stop talking, and documents are not shared. This is unfortunate. Conflict and disagreement are the clearest signs that more, not less, communication and information needs to be exchanged. Information and discussion, facts and ideas shared, are the raw material from which agreements emerge. Cutting the flow ensures conflict, delay, and lack of consensus about the outcome.

When working out issues or problems, full disclosure provides a blueprint for people to work with. Until everything is on the table, no one is dealing with the entire situation. Resolution involves breaking an old habit: instead of making sure your concerns are taken care of first, resolution incorporates the concerns of everyone at the same time.

Listening, understanding, and honoring others' concerns are critical in the process. Recognizing others' needs gets you what you want, and legitimizing their concerns sets up the conditions in which others can take care of your concerns.

Once "their" concerns are legitimized, they become your concerns too because they are concerns of the situation. Then solutions will more readily follow because you have people taking care of people, not people who have a position or people who want something. Taking care of others is natural for human beings. Compassion is the cornerstone of humanity.

9. Learning

Making agreements and creative resolution is essentially an exercise in group learning. The longer you can "listen" from a place of a "not knowing observer," the more comprehensive your solution will be. Keeping your mind open to learning facts, concerns, and perspectives of all people involved is essential.

Coming together to create an agreement or resolve a conflict, assuming commitment and the necessary attitude of resolution, is an exercise in group learning. Learning is a useful way to get rid of the ego-based ideas of winning, being right, fixing blame, or doing it the "right" way. Stepping into the perspective of learning and gathering information enables you to listen without defending or countering. While focused on winning, you may not want to know or listen to the concerns of other people. Your objective is to convince everyone you are right, no matter what. Learning puts you in a mind-set of discovery, allowing you the luxury of not knowing the answers or the specific path that you will take. This process lets you discover, explore, and learn with everyone else what the best solution is. As the process unfolds, everyone is educating each other about his or her situation, learning what is needed to understand the bigger picture.

Think of a group coming together with a set of desired outcomes. Everyone holds key information. No one knows the answer. By keeping the dialogue open the group arrives at an agreement in principle. In a team situation, everyone wants a fair resolution so they can get back to work. Through an open dialogue during which you learn about the others' particular concerns, you learn your way to what an effective agreement and resolution might look like.

10. Becoming Response Able

People abdicate personal responsibility for their deepest individual concerns when they avoid conflict. They stay clear of direct contact with others by delegating to "professionals"—managers, team leaders, executives, facilitators, counselors. This is done before they look within themselves for the answers. In fact, the more they engage in self-reflection and know about who they are, the better they can collaborate with others.

You may try to deal with the challenges of disagreement by giving it to professionals. You have been taught to believe they know how to do it right. But professionals can make you a spectator in your own situation by making you miss out on the discovery of your own internal and external boundaries, and the resolutions based on your own personal standards. More important, since the real source of conflict are the emotional reactions you have in situations, no one can resolve things for you as your emotional experience is highly subjective and very personal.

In resolving your own conflicts, you find out who you are, what your standards are, and the substance you are really made of. Under the Resolutionary Thinking paradigm, you remain the captain. You become "Response *Able*" when you deal with internal and external conflict. You get the direct experience of interacting with other people without professionals doing it for you. You get to engage with your own conflicts and collaborations.

Deferring to others dilutes the experience of discovering yourself. Personal identity is revealed as you observe your responses in dealing directly with difficult situations.

Resolutionary Thinking in Practice

Resolutionary Thinking is the context in which the art of resolution and agreement takes place. Thinking this way is an essential first step for effective, productive, powerful, and sustainable virtual collaborations.

Valuing Differences

The world is getting more global and multi-cultural every day and the lives and jobs affected by this shrinking of borders are ever expanding. At one time, "Diversity" was framed in terms of compliance, but now it has become a critical component of survival. Working in a diverse world forces those in it to be ready to have a diverse organization and remain mindful of the essential need for cultivating a diverse mind. Failure is the peril if society is unable to keep on this critical track.

Recognize Where You Are

Self-awareness is the foundation of emotional intelligence. As the working force collaborates across borders, collaboration with others emotional intelligence becomes a critical component of effectiveness and accomplishment. Having a healthy knowledge and sense of self is the place to begin, a place of foundation and ground for joint activity.

Creativity

Creativity bubbles up from the inside. It is not something to be willful about. The openness of Resolutionary Thinking enables the fertile ground that will yield fruit, both within you and among virtual colleagues. The opposite of boxed thinking enables unique talents to come through.

The Contribution of Your Natural Genius

Each member of society has a natural genius that does not come from one's background or education. It comes from a much deeper place that organizations and institutions would like to mine. It comes from who each individual member is. Every day millions of excellent workers, people who outside of their job run multi-million dollar businesses, and yet still are not afforded the opportunity to make their full contribution. When they arrive at the portal of their workplace, they don the constraining coat known as the "*Job Description.*" This coat tells them what they can and can't do regardless of their natural capacity or experience. In fact, organizations are begging for the full contribution of everyone on the payroll.

Reframing Organizational Politics

Organizational politics are a critical part of organizational participation. But politics has received a bad name. Of course there are good and bad political actors. But more important is the need to change the way people think about the political process of organizations. Organizations are inherently political bodies. And the politics of organizations is simply the sum of the conversations by which decisions are made about how the resources (including human) of the organization are used.

Building Bridges—"Third Body"

Teamwork, Synergy, Collaboration, and Creativity are all terms that deliver more than the sum of their parts. This can also be called the "*Third Body.*" When people join together effectively, an operational entity emerges that is Meta to each of the individuals. It's unpredictable and magical, but society's focus can expose the phenomenon and show how invigorating and productive it can be.

Qualities of a "Resolutionary"

The following characteristics summarize and embody Resolutionary Thinking. Can you embody them? Do you embody them?

Table 8: Qualities of a Resolutionary

Collaborative	Integrity
Common Sense	Intelligence
Confident	Judgment
Creative	Life Experience
Empathy	Listener
Fairness	Controls Process
Faith	To the Core
Conflict Tolerant	Cares for People
Models Openness	Practical

11 Creating Teams: 1.0 and 2.0

"Coming together is a beginning
Keeping together is progress
Working together is success"

—Henry Ford

A recent "Meetings Around the World" study surveyed 946 information technology and line-of-business decision-makers from a cross section of 2,000 small-to-medium, midmarket, and global companies in the U.S., Europe (France, Germany and the U.K.) and Asia-Pacific (Australia, Hong Kong and Japan). The researchers created a collaboration index to measure a company's relative collaborativeness:

Collaboration is a key driver of overall performance of companies around the world. Its impact is twice as significant as a company's aggressiveness in pursuing new market opportunities (strategic orientation) and five times as significant as the external market environment (market turbulence). Those are the results of a groundbreaking study "Meetings Around the World: The Impact of Collaboration on Business Performance" conducted by Frost & Sullivan and sponsored by Verizon Business and Microsoft Corp.

The study also showed that a global culture of collaboration exists, but that there are regional differences in how people in various countries prefer to communicate with one another. The results show that collaboration can positively impact each of the gold standards of performance: profitability, profit growth and sales growth to determine a company's overall performance in the marketplace. [31]

At this point in time, there are thousands of stories about the value of virtual collaboration technology. http://tinyurl.com/3ag6b7 is just one of many examples.

When speaking on collaboration in the virtual world, it is essential to talk about the formation of teams. Many of the traditional forces, processes, and metrics in the F2F world apply equally in the virtual world, the major differences being in the process by which people are engaged and connected, and how work is accomplished.

Advantages of Teams

Most people rush through life as if they had been shot out of cannon at about 8,000 miles an hour. They forget to remember some of the simple and fundamental benefits of working within a loose or highly structured collaboration. The following keys are intended as reminders of why working in collaboration with others is a valuable.

Increased individual commitment: When people work in large organizations it's their loyalty to other members of their team that serves as their primary motivation. People show up, participate, and perform their best because they know their colleagues are depending on them. It's rarely about the organizational mission—it's about the people and the team they work directly with, no matter how far or close. Relationships, trust, and interdependence are the product of working together toward an agreed goal.

Improved Quality, Productivity, Creativity, and Innovation: "All of us is smarter than any one of us!" When individuals collaborate with others, the group mind, if it can be accessed, is much smarter than a

---

31. Microsoft Press Pass, http://tinyurl.com/muama, June 2006.

single brain—it allows for many different perspectives and is connected to many social networks. That contributes to both what and how things get done.

Greater Job Satisfaction: For most people the social aspect of work is critically engaging. When connected in a collaborative environment the work becomes more enjoyable It has been demonstrated that many more people could telecommute but chose not to because they do not want to be deprived of the social relationships.

Enhanced Trust and Communication: When an individual is connected and communicating with a group of collaborators there is a spillover effect that permeates the mood and energy of the culture of an organization.

Characteristics of Real Teams

Team Size: Somewhere between 4 and 12 is the optimum number for a real team. Beyond 12 members, working together becomes unwieldy.

Common Goals and Rewards: In order to be a real team, the vision, goals, and metrics must be the same for every member of the team. It is essential that the structure support the sense of teamship. Straying from this structure and rewarding individual performance breaks down the sense of team. An essential component of developing collaborative teams is connecting people through shared accountability, rating, and rewards. Removing the ability to say "I did MY job" produces just the right kind of motivational "at-stakeness" that promotes true collaboration.

Decision Making: Since teams develop in the context of going after shared goals the team must be able to make decisions regarding the team when they are on the ground moving toward their goals. That is obviously an iterative process with the team members in the best place to make decisions as they move forward.

Team Formation

Involve Everyone: It is critical to involve all members of a virtual team in the planning and organizational process. Although this may take a little longer it will go a long way in reducing resistance. When people are told how they will work the inclination is to push back against an imposed structure. When people participate in determining how they will work, buy-in becomes a natural part of the process because they have direct input.

Training: Today's environment is characterized by a faster pace, competitive pressure, demanding internal and external customers, and data overloads. As multi-national presence grows, cost, time, and travel constraints increase. As technology improves, working virtually is becoming the prevailing fabric that knits organizations together. Because of the pace of change and resource constraints, there is a tendency to drop the training and learning component, leaving people to deal with change on their own.

Transitions would be more effective and less painful if people were given training to better understand their operating environment. Making this new way of working an "experiment" or a "learning experience" will go a long way toward taking the edge off for people. Creating the consciousness of a learning environment enables people to be more creative as they navigate new territory. Challenges, mistakes, and process improvements are much better mastered when they are seen as an accepted part of the territory.

Three kinds of training are essential:

- **Initial training:** Provide basic education in communication skills and collaborative process; assess to make sure people are with the program.

- **On-Demand training:** Use as needed to move through roadblocks

- **Continuous training:** Keeps people motivated

Resistance: It is essential to accept that some people will resist. The best way to get through this is to make team members aware so they can coach each other, have forums to discuss challenges, have outside resources available, and develop a set of personalized team best practices.

Trust: Time and experience when working with others builds trust. For a richer and deeper understanding of the phenomenon of trust the following two resources are quite useful.[32, 33]

Vision, Values and Themes: This helps cement people together in pursuit of agreed goals. Slogans, mottos, guidelines, and team processes and rules are essential to have.

Roles and Responsibilities: Who does what and how?

Team Agreements: Using the agreement template that follows helps ensure everyone is really on the same page.

Team Stages: Traditional teams go through the following four stages; these are the same for virtual teams:

1. **Forming:** The team comes together.

2. **Storming:** Conflict emerges about personality, work style, work process, communication skills, goals, meetings, resources, and measurements.

3. **Norming:** Moving through conflicts and developing norms for working together including socializing, team rules, team practices, team celebrations.

4. **Performing:** Getting work done effectively and efficiently.

A fifth stage is also quite relevant—**high performing**—teams aspire to step beyond merely performing into the realm of high performance.

---

32. Michele and Dennis Reina, *Trust and Betrayal in the Workplace*, 2nd Ed. (San Francisco: Berrett-Koehler 2006).
33. M.R. Covey, *The Speed of Trust* (Boston: Free Press, 2006).

The most important characteristic of teams that successfully step up to high performance is energy: Energy that is created by the appreciation, respect and even love that develops between team members as they work together. In the face-to-face world, that energy develops rather naturally through time spent together working in pursuit of common goals. It becomes a bit more challenging for those bonds to form in the virtual world. However, given the various tools available for all manner of collaboration, stepping up to the challenge certainly seems more than doable.

The expression, virtual happy hour, is a perfect term for this type of aura that one wants to create. Creating spaces for that kind of interaction though strange at first will contribute greatly to personal engagement. This obviously has a generational component that will make things easier over time.

Creating an Effective Team

Sierra Adoption Services is a private non-profit agency working in California. A key part of the Sierra mission is teaming with governmental agencies and supplementing the social services they provide for children in foster care. Sierra provides resources that are beyond government capacity, so that children who had been labeled "unadoptable" can be removed from the foster care system and placed in permanent adoptive families.

Sierra was working within a federally funded "partnership" known as "Capital Kids" with the child welfare agencies of the County of Sacramento, California. The working team between Sierra and Sacramento had fallen apart because of their history, and because they did not have a current, clear teaming agreement for results in place. It was discovered that there was a festering historical conflict. Sierra wanted to resolve both the long and short term conflict, get everyone beyond institutional mistrust, and forge an effective high-performance team. Very few people believed the working relationship was salvageable.

The initial meeting had nine members from the Sierra team and nine from Sacramento. The first half of the day was educational. Everyone was instructed in the dialog models for conflict resolution and agreements for results. The first models used facilitated the resolution of the existing conflict. This included uncovering the basis for past misunder-standings, and determining that it was possible to forge an effective team. Current concerns were revealed and a session was scheduled at which a team agreement was structured that provided the foundation for a solid, healthy, working relationships, and a new vision of partner-ship.

In the year following, the new team structure for a collaborative part-nership 109 children previously thought unadoptable, were placed in permanent adoptive homes. Here is the Sierra Adoption Services (SAS) agreement with Sacramento County (SC). Please note all the operational detail. It is in the detail of behavior that "collaboration" usually breaks down. That's why it's so important to take the time on the front end to pay attention to the details—the more detail, the more likely collaboration will take place.

CAPITAL KIDS OPERATIONAL AGREEMENT

1. INTENT &VISION: Our intention is to place as many kids as possible in permanent homes. The specific vision we have is:

- Become a model Public/Private Partnership—a shared culture of collaboration and agreement seen as a model for teaching others
- Place 150 kids next year
- SC provides 100 referrals/year to Sierra
- Positive stories about our working relationship are generated within agencies in the adoption community
- Sierra is accepted as a "resource" by the county
- Sierra makes the "challenging" jobs of Suzanne and Helen doable
- A transfer of knowledge and resources takes place such that SC learns how to use Sierra's methods and resources
- Funding flows easily because the results proved a high level of service
- People in both agencies want to be part of the program
- People at both agencies develop a high level of respect for each other
- People generate a 5:1 ratio of appreciations to complaint
- "Can't wait to go to work" attitude develops
- A presentation about the partnership is made at NACAC
- Partnering for performance is documented
- High level of fun, pride, and celebration

2. ROLES: We will be partners and resources for each other. SC will look to SAS to provide resources that are beyond their capacity or ability to provide.

3. PROMISES:

SC will:

- Identify children to be referred for the project.
- Obtain court permission to do child-specific recruitment.
- Provide full disclosure of child's risks and needs.
- Assure County representation at referral staffing meeting, including SC CapKids coordinator, long-term foster care worker and /or supervisor.
- Invite FFA worker if applicable.
- Upon request provide waiver of confidentiality to allow SAS worker to discuss child with child's therapist, FFA, Alta Regional Center, and other organizations and individuals as applicable.
- Inform current foster parent of the project.
- Facilitate SAS worker's introduction to the child, and team with SAS worker as appropriate.
- Child's worker will confer with SAS worker as needed re: adoptive families considered for placement, including concurrence with final placement choice. Families ruled out by SAS will be reported to SC worker.
- Assure Sacramento Capital Kids liaison to attend regularly scheduled joint staff meetings to review cases, exchange feedback, remove barriers to case moving forward, needs and services review, make new referrals, engage in dialogue necessary for project effectiveness.
- Assure that representatives will attend quarterly Advisory Board meetings.
- Foster Parent Adoption: a.) SAS will provide a home-study within four months. SC will provide information necessary for SAS to complete assigned foster parent home-studies. Unique situations will be processed on a case by case basis.
- Provide timely response to requests for documentation of placements, guardianships, and finalizations.
- Provide necessary assistance to make placement.
- Complete county requirements for adoptive placements within a reasonable time.
- Provide prompt AAP determination.
- Forward necessary documents to agency representing adopting family.
- Complete all necessary paperwork.
- Provide input for development of monthly project reports and quarterly grant progress reports.
- Participate in team-building activities and activities to identify and remove barriers.
- Participate in cross-training and joint-training activities.

- Disburse funds received from CDSS to SAS in accordance with grant budget.

SAS will:

- Provide training to SC project staff
- Review information on children referred and accepts or rejects the referral within 14 days
- Meet with foster parents of project children to explain project and gain cooperation. If foster parent decides to adopt and SC concurs with foster parent adoption provide home-study
- Conduct assessment of child's adoption needs. Assessment process will consist of a minimum of:
  - Meeting with child's worker
  - Review of Foster Child Summary, Child Available Form, CapKids
  - Referral Form, and psychological profile
  - Interviews with foster parent
  - Interviews with child
  - Interviews with other relevant individuals and organizations, as applicable
- Meet with child to prepare for recruitment process
- Facilitate photo and/or video session for the project
- Facilitate team approach with SC worker to help child reconcile his/her past and move forward to an adoption commitment
- Provide child-specific recruitment for each project child as necessary and as approved by juvenile court
- Provide placement services including
  - Assess and report to SC all interested families
  - Provide home-study's to appropriate families recruited to the project
  - Solicitation and review of appropriate home-study's from other licensed agencies
  - Confer with child's worker as needed re: adoptive families considered for placement, including concurrence with final placement choice
  - Interview families considered for placement
  - Oversee pre-placement visitation for children placed with SAS families
  - Facilitate placement process for children placed with SAS families
- In foster parent adoptions with foster families, SAS will provide a home-study within four months and unique situations will be staffed on a case by case basis
- Facilitate and attend regularly scheduled joint staff meeting with SC liaison

- to review cases, exchange feedback, and remove barriers to case moving forward
- to perform needs and services review, make new referrals, and
- to engage in dialogue necessary for project effectiveness
- Attend quarterly Advisory Board Meetings
- Develop monthly project reports and quarterly grant progress reports with the assistance of SC liaison
- Participate in team-building activities and activities to identify and remove barriers
- Participate in cross-training and joint-training activities

4. TIME & VALUE: We will assess our progress in six months. We agree that the effort we are devoting to this partnership is worth our time because of the potential value of finding permanent adoptive homes for the children.

5. MEASUREMENTS OF SATISFACTION: Placing 150 children in adoptive homes within one year.

6. CONCERNS AND FEARS:
   a. We will backslide to what was unworkable
   b. Each of us will be heard by the other as blaming and finding fault—in providing ongoing feedback, we either won't say the right things or we won't say anything
   c. People will forget forgiveness
   d. We will trigger each other
   e. Lack of effective feedback
   f. Not enough county resources
   g. Too many other demands for the project to work
   h. Won't be able to place 150 kids
   i. Suzanne will burn out
   j. We can't serve new kids

7. RENEGOTIATION / DISSOLUTION: We recognize that this is just the beginning of our partnership, and that we will likely have to modify our practices and this agreement as we operate within the structure we have designed. We know that developing a working relationship on this critical mission is most important, and we agree to continue to discover the best way to do that.

8. CONSEQUENCES: We understand that if we cannot work well together, many children will not be adopted into permanent families. For us, that is a huge consequence.

9. CONFLICT RESOLUTION: First we will talk, and then we will use Stewart's 7 Step Resolutionary model. If we can't resolve things at an operational level, we will ask our senior managers to facilitate. If that does not work, we will call Stewart Levine.

10. AGREEMENT: Yes, we are very satisfied with this new beginning.

Challenges to Collaboration 2.0

In Part I, the most common challenges to collaboration were detailed. Here are some responses. They may seem simplistic. They are not.

Resistance by people who are not well-versed in real collaboration which include:

- *We do not know each other*

  I have seen the agreement model used hundreds of times to create project plans between strangers.

- *We do not like each other*

  If you are committed to the vision, the model will enable you to begin working together. In that context, respect will develop

- *We do not understand each other*

  If you are committed to the vision, the model will enable you to begin working together. In that context, understanding develops.

- *We do not trust each other*

  If you are committed to the vision, the model will enable you to begin working together. In that context, trust develops.

- *Our virtual meetings are going sideways*

  If you are committed to the vision, the model will enable you to begin working together. In that context, you can develop agreements about how you will work together and how meetings will be run.

- *We do not know how to resolve conflicts*

  If you are committed to the vision, the model will enable you to begin working together. Chapter 14 contains a model for moving through conflicts. Conflicts are an ordinary, expected part of collaboration.

- *Participation in meetings*

  If you are committed to the vision the model will enable you to begin working together. In that context you can develop agreements about how everyone will participate in meetings.

- *Making decisions*

  If you are committed to the vision the model will enable you to begin working together. Making decisions are a subset of resolving conflict which the model addresses.

- *Hidden agendas*

  If you are committed to the vision the model will facilitate the surfacing of concerns and fears about hidden agendas and enable people to have an authentic conversation about perceived hidden agendas. As people embrace a win/win attitude they recognize that with creativity everyone can win. No one needs to lose.

- *Lack of clear direction*

  If you are committed to the vision the model will enable you to begin working together and will always enable you to renegotiate so you have a clear vision and direction.

- *Lack of follow-up and a consistent communication loop*

  A team leader or project manager is responsible for keeping the project on track and communicating what is going on. That is their role.

- *Protocols for communicating outside the team*

  You get to make them up.

Solution: Beginner's Mind!!!

With good initial training and ongoing dialogue about people, process, and technology, the collaboration will usually come together. One critical fact is having some patience. In situations involving new relationships, it takes some time to develop a way of working together and gain knowledge of each other. There is a learning curve for any new activity. It just takes some commitment to keep getting up after you fall down.

12 The Law and Principles of Agreement

"The time of the lone wolf is over. Gather yourselves! Banish the word struggle from your attitude and your vocabulary. All that we do must now be done in a sacred manner and in celebration. We are the ones we've been waiting for."—Oraibi, A Hopi elder

Before sharing the elements of "Agreements for Results," it is important to understand the truths behind them. Laws and Principles are universal truths that are difficult to push back against.

The *Law of Agreement* and the *Principles of Agreement* are fundamental truths. Although they are simple and obvious, the challenge is to apply and follow them. *The Law and Principles are simple to understand, but they are not always easy to implement.*

Table 9:   Law and Principles of Agreement[34]

Law of Agreement
Every collaboration is established in language by making implicit (talking to yourself about what you think the agreement is) and explicit (discussing agreement with others) agreements.
Principles of Agreement
1. *The source of all productivity and fulfillment in personal and professional relationships is effective collaboration. The more elegant the expression of the collaboration the better the results will be.*
2. *Society works and lives in a sea of agreements.*
3. *Most individuals never learned the essential elements of an effective agreement.*
4. *Clear agreements empower. They express a shared vision and a path to desired results.*
5. *Clear agreements improve the chances for satisfaction. They set up the conditions that produce delighted customers, teammates, colleagues, vendors, and family members.*
6. *Practice enables you to craft masterful agreements.*
7. *Collaboration and agreement for results is simple, but it is not easy. It requires thoughtfulness and clear thinking on the front end before you move into action, and a commitment to get through the rough spots after you begin.*
8. *No matter how clear and complete the agreement everything will not be addressed—conflicts and differences will arise that you must be prepared to resolve.*
9. *Breakdowns are not a cause for alarm, they are to be an expected opportunity for creativity.*
10. *Resolving conflicts leads to new agreements.*

34. Stewart Levine, *The Book of Agreement* (San Francisco: Berret-Koehler, 2002).

Understanding the Law and Principles of Agreement

Law of Agreement

Every collaboration is established in language by making implicit (talking to yourself about what you think the agreement is) and explicit (discussing agreement with others) agreements.

When you form a partnership with someone, take a job in a large organization, get married, buy a product, or go out for the evening, it involves coordinating your actions. Sometimes detailed agreements with others are written—leases, licensing contracts, business partnerships and executive employment contracts, and sometimes not. When lawyers get involved they start imagining things that might go wrong. They try to protect from the "what ifs"—what if this goes wrong, or what if that goes wrong. They try to make the "what ifs" explicit and then move forward to protect against whatever they can. What often happens in the name of protection is they foster an adversarial relationship at the beginning—exactly what a new collaboration does not need.

More important than the clarity of the agreement is the quality of the relationship that develops both before and during the partnership. Lasting success is not about the agreement—it's the relationship that flows from the collaboration. When you have the same vision of a desired result, everyone is working toward making that vision a reality.

If you do not discuss the specific understanding with the other person or group, the agreement is implicit. The potential for difficulty is that different people will have a different implicit understanding of their agreement. This is usually the root of conflict.

The Principles

1. The source of all productivity and fulfillment in personal and professional relationships is effective collaboration. The more elegant the expression of the collaboration the better the results will be.

You can examine your life and the culture you live in for evidence of this truth. Organizations are reflections of the collaborative efforts of many. Management and leadership are about coordinating others' efforts like conducting a great symphony. This is true for marriages, friendships, families, and organizational teams. In any context, the tighter the coordination, the more effective the end results because of the greater level of synergy.

Think of the coordination between spouses in a highly functional marriage. That same level of effective coordination is present in a business partnership, work team, department, or organization. Effective coordination yields a quadratic expansion of productivity. It is dependent on the clarity of agreements.

The second critical aspect of agreements is their impact on personal and professional relationships. Most satisfaction in both personal and professional lives depends on the quality of interpersonal relationships: the clearer the agreements, the deeper and more satisfying the relationships. Everyone knows where he or she is going—no one is holding back. All of their energy is in the "game" of producing results, not fighting insignificant battles. The opposite is equally true. Without clear agreements coordination is missing, productivity is diminished and suffering and conflict becomes pervasive.

Most conflict resolution consulting work involves getting everyone to operate under the same vision. The main thing missing is a shared vision of what people are supposed to accomplish together. Conflict develops because this was not clearly expressed before everyone moved into action. Agreements are the context in which all activity happens.

Virtual teams demand a clear expression of the desired outcome and plan for getting there.

You can look at your life as a series of agreements. Try viewing your life through a "lens of agreement." Most everything in your life is governed by the set of expectations you have as a result of the explicit and implicit agreements. These include:

- Those with the spouse you share your life with.

- The soldiers that protect your national borders.

- The utility companies that supply electricity, water and gas.

- The market that sells you breakfast food.

- The manufacturer of your clothing.

- The municipality that provides police protection and picks up your trash.

- The day care center where you leave your youngest child.

- The station that services your car and sells you gasoline.

- The school board that educates your children.

- The company that pays your salary.

- The boss you work for.

- The company that services your computer.

- The restaurant where you eat lunch.

- The garage you park your car in all day.

- The babysitter who took care of your kids.

- The pizza parlor that delivers dinner.

3. Most individuals never learned the essential elements of an effective agreement.

Because collaboration is such a primary life skill it is hard to believe that early schooling did not teach most folks about collaboration. As youngsters people might have learned how to construct an effective agreement. When people are given the opportunity to learn a model for crafting collaborative agreements audiences get enthusiastic.

Unfortunately, the way most get better at crafting explicit agreements is when they suffer because their agreements are ineffective. This makes people cautious and distrustful, hindering clarity and the ability to get beyond the troubled past. Unfortunately unless one shifts their way of thinking the more paranoid and protective they will become, which can be very ineffective.

4. Clear agreements empower and express a shared vision and a path to desired results.

When an agreement contains the needs and vision of everyone involved an opportunity is presented to express a powerful shared vision for the project. It is imperative that a detailed picture of the result be visualized so that everyone will be pleased with the outcome. It's not about you OR me; it's about you AND me! A clear agreement provides a clearly expressed shared vision and the path to making it a reality. It details the promises essential to achieving the desired result. The agreement manages the "project," as a map that empowers and enrolls everyone in producing the shared vision—the composite of all the personal visions.

5. Clear agreements improve the chances for satisfaction. They set up the conditions that produce delighted customers, teammates, colleagues, vendors and family members.

A huge amount of suffering takes place because there is an unclear or lack of an explicit agreement. In unclear situations most people don't know what to do, don't know the results expected of them, and/or what they can expect of others. This causes fear and anxiety. If you take the time at the outset to express where you are headed, the route of travel, and who will do what to get you to the destination, everyone would know how their needs will be taken care of. They would also know what to do to fulfill their promises.

Recall the Quaker State commercial "You can pay me now and have your oil changed, or you can pay me much later for costly engine repairs!" It's the same way with agreements—you can take the time at the beginning and prevent the potential of a costly hassle later on. It is that simple! And, it is hard work to change life long thinking and behavioral habits.

6. Practice enables you to craft masterful agreements.

Working with a new model is challenging. Everyone wants instant success. Even a novice skier wants to take on the black diamond on their initial run. Most people either want to master that new software program or move on. If people stay patient within a short time the essential elements of the agreement template will become internalized. After a while you will be making sure that you have effective agreements in place for all of the important aspects of your life. You will be growing your ability to craft effective "Agreements for Results." Be patient, allow yourself to step into the "beginner's mind." Let time and experience be your teacher. You will become artful with the use of the template. Obviously, not every situation requires an explicit agreement, and, not every situation requires the "religion" of a 10 element agreement. But, you must start with learning the basics.

7. Collaboration and agreement for results is simple, but it is not easy. It requires thoughtfulness and clear thinking on the front end, and a commitment to get through the rough spots after you begin.

Periodically, a legislator proposes more stringent requirements for a marriage license. Principle 7 makes a similar suggestion—it is a reminder that doing something effectively with another person is not easy, and can become especially difficult if you don't pay attention to the details on the front end. Just as important is not to be surprised when you begin and conflicts you did not anticipate come up.

8. No matter how clear and complete the agreement everything will not be addressed—conflicts and differences will arise and you must be prepared to solve them.

No matter how much time you spend or how thorough you are, you will not think of everything. If you are doing something no one has done before, you will not be able to predict all the parameters. You will have to revisit things you did not think about, and circumstances you did not foresee. Although you can prevent and reduce conflict, you cannot eliminate it. In some sense, it is important to remember that being "in the process of moving toward clear agreement" is where most time will be spent and rarely is time spent on the cusp of a perfect agreement. Your goal is to "normalize" conflict while developing a healthy and friendly relationship with it.

When flying from New York to San Francisco, the plane is "dead on course" about 5% of the time. The remainder of the time, the pilot is making course corrections. That's the way it is. Learn to enjoy "being in the process". It is a great gift because that's where most people spend the majority of their lives. This is why an essential element of every agreement is a process for resolving inevitable conflicts.

9. Breakdowns are not a cause for alarm, they are to be an expected opportunity for creativity.

Conflict and resolution are part of the same cycle. Like republicans and democrats, and the fluctuation of the Dow, breakdowns (a stop in the action moving toward desired outcomes) are a blessing. They provide the opportunity to look at the situation with fresh eyes. From the current perspective you have the luxury of more up to date information from which to act. Hold the context as one of on-going learning as you work with someone or a group. When things go wrong do your best not to blame, find fault, and prove yourself right or them wrong. At this juncture, it is imperative that the next step be about what happened so you can fix the difficulty and improve the entire process for the next time you begin. Remember, most conflict is structural, not intentional.

How people think about situations sets the context and helps create the mind map that governs how an individual or group will process and experience situations. A book by Wayne Dyer, Ph.D., called "Gifts from Eykis," his only book of fiction, sets the tone for this type of situation. It's the story of a woman named Eykis who visits planet earth from a sister planet far out in the universe. As she tours planet earth, she becomes increasingly upset by the amount of suffering she observes. What really bothers her is that most of the suffering is caused by how people are conditioned to think about things. Through the eyes of Eykis it can be seen that when things go wrong, the knee jerk reaction is to blame, find fault or punish someone or something who the consensus believes to be at fault. Where Eykis came from, the most important inquiry was "how can we prevent this from happening again."[35]

10. Resolving conflicts leads to new agreements

The end result of any conflict resolution process is a new agreement determining what the relationship will be in the future. This has two important implications:

1. By taking time at the beginning of new professional relationships (teams, joint ventures, employment contracts), a great deal of suffering and conflict can be prevented.

2. When conflict arises, the best thing to do is to devote one's energy to looking to the future, and the desired results, and ask what must take place to get you there. That will guide you to a new agreement. Remember, it is only useful to look at past behavior to improve the future, not to affix blame.

The goal that all organizations must set is that, when people get into difficulty they can say to each other "this is not working, is it?" They must realize that the quickest way to fix the situation is to figure out what is not working about the present agreement—what is incomplete

---

35. Wayne Dyer, Ph.D., *Gifts from Eykis*, (New York: Simon & Schuster, 1983).

about the process, or who is not doing what they are supposed to and why? Next step—make a new agreement and let the situation go. No drama, no fault, no blame, nor punishment.

Just a new agreement!

13 Creating Agreements for Results

> "Multiple realities inform each other, fertilize, stimulate, and stir the cauldron of creativity."
> —David La Chapelle

It is much easier not to exercise or brush your teeth in the morning. It is much simpler just to get on with your day. Although stopping to form an agreement before moving forward is more tedious than moving into action immediately, it will not likely produce the results you desire. It's the difference between

"Ready – Fire – Aim!"

and

"Ready – Aim – Fire!"

Aiming before firing is much more effective because it provides clear direction before action. This is true for all collaborative activities. When introducing the concept of **Agreements for Results** to an audience, the tag line from an old Quaker State Motor Oil commercial once again comes into play:

"You can pay me now, or you can pay me later."

That line holds true when thinking about agreements. Most people never think about investing the time to make explicit the implicit agreement they believe they have at the beginning of a new professional relationship, team, or project. They're off and running, everyone with their own vision of the destination, and how to get there, without the clarity necessary to minimize the potential for conflict. Like the Quaker State warning of engine damage, if you don't do the preventative maintenance of changing your oil, the cost that will be incurred is inevitable conflict, which is a cost that can be prevented.

When most people think about the idea of having an *agreement* they usually think about long legal documents, lots of "what ifs" and "how we can protect ourselves from something we do not want to happen". People would be better off if, when beginning a new endeavor they could shift their focus to a vision of results they want to produce, not the calamities they want to avoid.

The following *Ten Essential Elements*[36] make up the template of items that must be discussed if you want to create a vision and a map to getting the results everyone wants. I then compare the mindset of an "Agreements for Results" perspective, with the traditional "Agreements for Protection" mental model. Notice the difference and think about which one is more effective.

---

36. Stewart Levine, *The Book of Agreement,* (San Francisco: Berret-Koehler, 2002).

Chapter 13: Creating Agreements for Results

Essential Elements

1. **Intent & Vision:** Big picture of what you want. The clearer and more specific the desired outcomes, the more likely you will succeed as visualized.

2. **Roles:** The duties, responsibilities, and commitment of everyone you need to achieve the desired results.

3. **Promises:** Promises of action steps. Specific commitments tell you if the actions will get you to the desired results, and what actions are missing.

4. **Time & Value:** All promises have "by-whens" and the timeframe during which the agreement will be effective. Is the exchange fair and does it provide enough incentive?

5. **Measurements of Satisfaction:** The evidence you achieved for your objectives must be clear, direct, and measurable to eliminate conflict about whether you accomplished what you began.

6. **Concerns & Fears:** Unspoken difficulties need to be expressed and the fear behind them addressed. This deepens understanding of what you are taking on, and the partnership you are creating with yourself.

7. **Renegotiation:** No matter how optimistic and clear it will become necessary to renegotiate promises and conditions of satisfaction because things change. The quality of working relationships is more important than anything.

8. **Consequences:** Know the consequences for breaking promises, and what will be lost if the project is not completed.

9. **Conflict Resolution:** Conflicts and disagreements will arise. Agree to an "attitude of resolution," and an agreed-upon resolution process.

10. **Agreement:** When you have reflected on 1 through 9, ask whether you "trust" moving forward. Do not move into action unless and until you can say *YES* and commit to embracing the future as an opportunity to be enjoyed.

The model draws out both the vision and the road map to it. It provides a path to what you want to accomplish. Making an agreement with your collaborators is an excellent way of framing the working relationship!

Table 10: Agreements for Results vs. Protection

Results vs. Protection Focus Comparison		
	Results Focus	**Protection Focus**
Intent & Vision	Desired outcome	What-ifs
Roles	Take responsibility	Limit accountability
Promises	Commitment	Qualifiers and conditioners
Time & Value	By-whens / fair return	Most for least
Measurements of Satisfaction	Inspiring goals	Excuses and escapes
Concerns & Fears	Compassion / understanding	Edge for strategic advantage
Renegotiation	Deal with unknowns / changes	Strike hard bargain
Consequences	Reminder of promises	Punishment
Conflict Resolution	Get back on track	Exact some premium
Agreement	Trust enough	Escape possible?

Agreements for Results vs. Protection

1. Intent & Vision

Focus on what you want to have happen, not on all the "what ifs" that could go wrong.

You can tell what will happen in your life by paying attention to your dominant thoughts. If an individual focuses on the calamities, then they increase their chances of the calamity taking place. What is needed in any collaborative context is for everyone to focus on desired results—the best possible vision of the future. That will greatly improve the chances of materializing what is needed and wanted to happen. It is obvious that when you bring on a new hire, it is more useful to see them leaping tall buildings than focusing on the mistakes they might make.

2. Roles

Who takes responsibility for all critical tasks without limiting accountability?

All groups, corporations, and individuals want to make sure they have what they need to get the job done without anything slipping through the cracks. They want clarity around who can be counted on for what, compared to taking the position of "That's not my job!" In the old context people liked to hide. They did not like to take the responsibility for making something happen because if something went wrong, they were responsible. The fear of making mistakes is no longer as powerful a driver it once was. Most have learned that the need for innovation requires experimentation. They know that mistakes cannot be "punished" when dealing with intrapreneurship and entrepreneurship.

3. Promises

Based on their belief in the project's mission, what type of unqualified, wholehearted contribution does each person need to perform to ensure its success?

Who specifically will be doing what? Consider this a project management plan. This is also a checkpoint—if everyone delivers what he or she promises, will you produce the desired results? Each promise must have the discipline of a "by when," because without a date commitment the promise is illusory.

4. Time & Value

Clear time commitments and stated satisfaction with the value given and received.

Clearly state "by-whens" and indications of how long the promises will be kept: Everyone must be satisfied that what they will get from the project is worth what they are putting in. If someone is under-compensated, they will be resentful. Resentful participants do not produce results that are "beyond expectation," but people committed to a vision do.

5. Measurements of Satisfaction

Goals that inspire and state clearly and measurably what is expected.

What are the objective measures that will tell you if you accomplished what you set out to do so that there are no arguments about it? For some people, it is frightening to make a commitment that will hold them visibly accountable to a promise they made, so they will look for an edge.

6. Concerns & Fears

Expressing any "anxiety-producing" concerns and risks so a "partner" can respond.

You address concerns and fears to make everyone as comfortable as possible about moving forward. Doing this is a way of responding to "internal chatter" that might inhibit full participation. It solidifies partnership by addressing what is lingering in people's minds. It enables people to clearly identify risks, and to choose to move forward anyway. Each person should be willing to take the other's deal.

7. Renegotiation

Collaborative iterations as unanticipated changes come up without taking advantage.

A commitment to renegotiation requires ongoing learning, and staying in a mindset of solving a mutual problem to get desired results even though things happened that no one anticipated (which you can count on). This is the key principal that drives every learning organization.

8. Consequences

Expressing the significance of promises and all impacts of failing to achieve the vision.

It is important to keep people mindful of promises they made and focused on delivering promised performance. It is as important to have people realize the connection between their expectations and failure to perform. Becoming conscious of that gap serves as a motivator. Consequences are put in place not as punishment, but to remind the contributors of the loss of an unrealized vision and the sanctity of promises.

9. Conflict Resolution

How can we get back on track quickly without inconveniencing anyone?

It is important to embrace conflict as expected and to consider it an opportunity for creativity in how one deals with the specifics of what one did not anticipate. It is very important to understand the magnitude of the transaction cost of remaining in conflict.

10. Agreement

Does everyone trust enough to be in an open, ongoing collaboration?

Has the process produced enough trust so you can say, "Let's do it! I'm comfortable moving forward with you, and I have a sense that we'll be able to work things out as we go forward." Has the deep dialogue that has been exchanged produced what Max DePree calls, "a relationship based on covenant—a heart felt connection and commitment to people and results?"[37]

Agreements are a fundamental life skill we never learned as adolescents. It is the primary building block for all kinds of collaborations and working with others and is the only way results, productivity, and satisfying relationships take place. Try having a dialogue that incorporates the elements at the beginning of your next project. It is almost guaranteed that you will become an advocate for "Agreements for Results" in all endeavors.

The critical part of a successful team environment is making sure everyone has the same vision, before moving into action. The classic "forming, storming, norming, performing" stages,[38] that teams traverse are best resolved with an agreement. The agreement serves the norming function as members of the team agree on how they will work with each other, what their norms will be. The agreement reflects the resolution of their "storming." An example of a team agreement by a government agency follows.

Based on this agreement, team members reported that they enjoyed the process, found that dialogue generated closer relationships and they used their agreement to orient new team members. The agreement has become a combination of an operations and personnel manual for the team.

---

37. Max DePree, *Leadership is an Art* (New York: Bantam Doubleday Dell, 1989).

38. B.W. Tuckman, Developmental Sequence in Small Groups. *Psychological Bulletin*, Vol. 63, 1965, pp. 384-399.

The Team Agreement

1. INTENT & VISION: All members of "The Programmers" agree to follow the terms of this agreement. Our vision is to be a tightly coordinated unit whose members are cross-trained in the jobs that all members of the team can do, so that any one of us could step into a client request at any moment. The specific vision we have is that we will be "self-supporting" within two years. We will generate enough revenue to cover our costs and our salaries. We will:

- Train each other in what we do;

- Become competent salespeople;

- Sell our core competencies to other government and non-government agencies;

- Become a role model for what an intrapreneurial government agency can do;

- Become qualified experts in providing programming support for the growing technology business community;

- Pool our resources so that some of us will become salespeople while others will be engaged in direct, immediate revenue opportunities.

2. ROLES: We will each become intrapreneurs, life-long learners, teammates, and a "work-family" that realizes that we are each essential to the others' survival during a time of government and military downsizing. We realize a cooperative management team and a steady stream of new solvent clients is critical to our success.

3. PROMISES: We each promise to:

- Accept rewards on a team basis only

- Give each other ongoing honest feedback on matters that impact our work and productivity

- Accept that we are beginners in the realm of interpersonal communication

- To devote our full time energy to the work of the team

- Teach teammates what we learn when we take a training class

- Come to team meetings on time

- Follow the standards for team meetings we have drafted

- Stay in a learning mode

- Take our turn as team-leader

4. TIME & VALUE: We each agree that the potential benefits of teamship far outweigh the costs involved, and we agree to experiment with the team method of organizing work for the next two years.

5. MEASUREMENTS OF SATISFACTION: Our measure of success will be sustainability—how long it takes to become self-sustaining. We have set a goal of 18 months to become self-supporting: revenue equals expenses plus salaries.

6. CONCERNS & FEARS: We are concerned that in six months a new "management" fad will be put in place, or we will be reassigned to other units and our operation will be completely shut down. We are also concerned that members of the team will leave for other departments or non-government jobs.

7. RENEGOTIATION: We understand the importance of ongoing communication. In that spirit, we see our team agreement as a living, evolving context in which we work together. We agree to keep our agreement current; we will look at it monthly to make sure it reflects the reality of what we are doing as a unit. We see "teamship" as a voluntary activity and agree that if anyone wants to leave the team they can.

8. CONSEQUENCES: We assume that all of us are smarter than any one of us. We agree to defer to the team to determine consequences for any violation of this team agreement. We realize that when we violate an expressed or implied responsibility of teamship, a consequence should follow. We fully understand that if we are not successful at becoming self-sustaining our unit may be disbanded and we will be left without jobs.

9. CONFLICT RESOLUTION: We agree to the following rules:

- Manage your own emotions
- Talk to the person or group you are in conflict with
- Ask a team member to mediate
- Get the entire team involved
- Ask the team coach for help

10. AGREEMENT: We are confident that all of us working together are stronger than we would be if we worked independently during this time of change and transition. We all take responsibility for managing the team as we rotate team leadership.

14 Productivity and the Cycle of Resolution

> *"The key to navigating the storms of turbulence cannot be found in any tool or device. The sum of our relationships will establish the overall health of our vessels and their journeys. Hence, an ethic of care and compassion for others is as fundamental as any other tool as we set out on our travels."*—David La Chapelle

Resolution can be as simple as letting go of the conflict without the need to process it at length, and crafting a new agreement. In fact, the compelling characteristic of high performing teams is the competence to quickly move through conflicts that come up. Be it wisdom, maturity, or focus high performance comes from getting out of one's own way and doing the work.

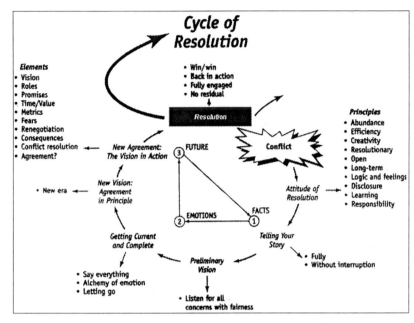

Figure 31: The Cycle of Resolution[39]

Table 11:   The Resolution Process

The Resolution Process
1. Attitude of Resolution – New thinking about conflict/agreement
2. Telling the Story* – Everyone's uninterrupted turn to speak
3. Preliminary Vision – The focus on what would be fair to everyone
4. Current and Complete* – Letting go and leaving the past behind
5. Agreement in Principle – What is the new relationship
6. New Agreement* – Details and plan for the new relationship
7. Resolution – In action and productivity without "chatter"
* Conversational action steps described in this chapter.

39. Stewart Levine, The Change Handbook, (San Francisco: Berrett-Koehler, 2007), Ch. 52.

Conversational Step 1: Telling Your Story

You begin getting the facts on the table when you start telling your story and listening to all stories, including yours. It is about understanding and being understood, one of the Seven Habits of Highly Effective People that Dr. Steven Covey inspires us to cultivate.[40] If you learn to listen with a careful ear and honor everyone's story about a situation, you take a big step toward getting to resolution.

Listening for a Preliminary Vision of Resolution

As you are listening, it is imperative that you start thinking about a resolution that honors all concerns in the situation. It is about shifting from the desire to win and getting your way to a vision that everyone can buy into. It comes from a sense of fairness. This initial vision may change as you gather more information and learn more.

Conversational Step 2: Dealing with the Emotion: Getting Current and Complete

This step can demand saying difficult things. It is about articulating what usually goes unexpressed and escaping from the emotional and intellectual prisons that keep us locked in the past. It is a way to face the good and bad in any situation and to experience and grieve for the disappointment of unrealized expectations. It is a way to put all of the detail out on the table—and choose those remnants that can be used to weave a new tapestry of resolution. These are the really courageous conversations. For a detailed description of the conversational process, please see Chapter 18 of *Getting to Resolution*.

Seeing a Vision for the Future: Agreement in Principle

Having looked at what other people need and noticing the cracks in your righteous position, you are ready to reach a general understanding of the resolution. This is the foundation of a new agreement. You let go of the desire for what you know will not work, and you focus on what will. This is a broad brush stroke vision of the future.

---

40. Steven Covey, *Seven Habits of Highly Effective People,* (New York: Simon & Schuster, 1989).

Conversational Step 3: Crafting the New Agreement: Making the Vision into Reality

It is time to put specifics onto the agreement in principle. You design and construct a detailed vision of the future using the "Agreement For Results" template. You have a map, a formula for the dialogue that will maximize the potential for everyone to obtain their desired results. The more time you spend in detailing the desired results, the greater the chance to realize them.

Resolution: When Your Agreement Becomes Reality

The final step is moving back into action. With a new agreement and a quiet, clear mind about the past, you can freely move forward, devoting your energy and intention to currently desired outcomes. You will have a new and profound sense of freedom because you have spoken on everything that needs to be said. You have completed the past and constructed a clear picture of the future and of the highway that will get you there. You will be empowered by the process. *You are resolved.*

Theory to Practice

I have been using the models and templates described above for almost twenty years in diverse applications for myself and with clients. I originally developed them in the context of serving as a divorce mediator. My thesis: if they work here, they will work anywhere. I am pleased to report that my thesis was correct. I migrated the application to business partnerships, law firms, joint ventures, hospitals, trade associations, consulting organizations, government agencies, and global corporations. The conversational templates for agreement and resolution have been introduced and used successfully, among many others, in the following environments:

- World Bank Office of Mediation
- American Management Association
- Project Management Institute
- US Treasury Department Executive Institute
- US Navy

- NASA Speaker Series Colloquium
- Booz Allen Hamilton
- Defense Research Institute
- American Bar Association
- Honda
- Washington DC Government and Law Department

Twenty five years ago, I had a vision for how people might collaborate more effectively through agreement and conflict resolution templates. At the time, my vision was limited by existing technology. The vision as formed in the early 1980's was to have Kiosks in all neighborhoods staffed by people who could quickly help people work together more effectively when conflict occurred. If you were in trouble, you could quickly access expert advice. Today, that is eminently possible because of where technology has taken us. In effect, everyone who wants one has a "Kiosk" on their desktop that can serve as an oracle that fosters collaboration. The way I see this all working from a communications perspective is a vision with the following elements:

- All technology "collaboration" tools have interpersonal skills tutorials. You don't get to use the technology until you demonstrate a level of communication competence.

- Before you begin a project you must complete an agreement about what you are all doing together. An agreement template doc is part of the technology.

- If you get into conflict, the technology would have the capacity to guide you through a process that gets you to resolution.

- Organizations would have a cadre of "virtual facilitation" coaches and such expertise would be part of the standard skill set of every facilitator who when initially engaged would consider the assignment and design to process with the least carbon and human impact.

In fact, that vision already exists in the way I personally operate. In hundreds of situations, I have been able to bring people to agreement at the beginning of projects and through conflict when needed from the comfort of my office using very basic webinar technology. I have recently created a web-based program that teaches the models in this book and facilitates creating agreements and resolving conflict. In beta testing, it has been used successfully in a number of different applications. I have also used virtual technology to guide 18 people through a twelve week course called "Becoming a Resolutionary" using the electronic technology. I'm looking forward to more widespread application!

15 Collaborative Evolution in the Enterprise

People resist change, and organizations resist change to an exponentially greater degree!" A corollary to this law is: *"The larger the organization, the greater the change, or the more complex the project, the greater the exponent for the resistance to change."*—Coleman's Law by David Coleman

Over the last 17 years, Collaborative Strategies (CS) has worked with a wide variety of organizations adopting collaboration technologies. Many of these were "early adopter" groups in larger companies, who were pioneers and had to deal with the pitfalls of new technologies. But now that collaboration technologies are about 30 years old, they are moving more into the mainstream, with some of these technologies already being commoditized. The goal of this chapter is to look at the various stages that organizations go through in adopting collaborative software and deploying it successfully throughout the enterprise. A secondary goal of this chapter is to help you determine where your organization is.

It is important to look at the adoption of collaboration technologies from a holistic point of view and look at: people, process and technology. Assessment tools, metrics, and strategies to help organizations move to a greater level of success and adoption of collaborative technologies are critical parts of this process and help to ensure that organizations can reap the rewards they envision.

The 5 Steps in Collaborative Technology Adoption

Table 12 shows the five stages for adopting collaborative technologies in organizations.

Table 12: The Five Stages in Collaborative Technology Adoption

Stages of Adoption	Collaborative Technologies		
Stage 1: Traditional Collaboration	Telephone	Face-to-Face meetings	E-mail, phone, fax, other classic technologies
Stage 2: Specific Problems and Applications	Audio, Video, and Data Conferencing	EIM, IM, Chat, and presence detection	Virtual team Spaces (VTS)
Stage 3: Collaborative Proliferation	Multiple A/V/D conferencing tools	Yahoo, MSN, AOL, Google	Groove, eRoom, WebOffice, etc.
Stage 4: Consolidation and Standardization	Standardize on SIP/Simple or XMPP	One client for all IM clouds	Common Virtual Team Space for everyone
Stage 5: Virtual Work Environment	Standard Tools in Place	Integration with mobile environments	Standard desktop and Web interface for anyone

Stage 1: Traditional Collaboration

As most organizations grow, they don't have a well thought out communications strategy or plan in place. They grow organically and use traditional technologies or processes, such as the telephone with voice mail, audio conferencing, face-to-face meetings, e-mail, fax, and services like FedEx.

These types of technologies have been used extensively over the last twenty years by people in their daily work lives. However, some of these technologies do not work well in collaborative situations. For example, voice calls can be very cumbersome when the parties are trying to share complex or graphic information with each other. Fax is OK for transmitting graphics, but it is not in color, which may convey misleading or confusing information to the recipient. E-mail does not let you detect the presence of someone you want to interact with now, nor does the phone on your desk. There may be a significant lag time before you connect with the other person. It is not a good idea to break up with your girlfriend over e-mail. E-mail is great to set up an appointment or give the status of a task or project, but it carries no emotional tone, and so is the wrong communications tool for something as personal and emotional as ending a relationship.

Phone, fax, and e-mail as communications tools all have limitations, especially when dealing with groups of people.

Stage 2: Specific Application

As people realize the collaborative tools on their desk do not support the level of information and contextual interaction they really need, it can become "every man for himself." Individual business units and departments seek out and find collaborative solutions that address their specific business processes or problems. However, since they only have control over a specific team or group, the solution is often isolated within that group, forming silos of collaboration within the organization.

Stage 3: Collaborative Proliferation

As awareness of collaboration solutions expands to other parts of the organization, additional solutions and services may be implemented, adding to the proliferation. Unfortunately, IT, which may have had little or no say in selecting these solutions, often finds itself facing potential security risks and having to support many different and competing collaboration technologies across the enterprise, which can be very costly. For example, Oracle was using eleven different Web conferencing solutions before they developed their own commercial application and implemented it internally across the enterprise.

Stage 4: Consolidation

At some point, IT takes control of the proliferation issue and starts an initiative to consolidate the collaboration technologies into as few solutions as possible. The different collaboration tools being used by the various business units and departments are often very similar in functionality. A consolidation program is initiated that involves developing a common set of collaboration requirements among the various business units. These requirements are used to evaluate and select a vendor solution that best meets the overall needs of the enterprise. Pilot projects are used to implement the chosen solution in selected groups and validate that it meets requirements before being rolled out to the rest of the enterprise. In this stage, the issue is more about people and process than about technology.

During the rollout process, the focus is on metrics, productivity, and iteration. Usage of the collaborative solution is measured including the number of users, number of meetings, number of minutes, etc. This provides insights on adoption of the technology.

Stage 5: Virtual Work Environment

After the rollout process, the focus shifts to expanding the reach and optimizing the collaborative value network, both internally and externally with customers, suppliers, partners, etc. The flow and value of information being passed between people when they interact is analyzed and used to eliminate bottlenecks and increase content value. Collaborative solutions are more tightly integrated with critical business processes and applications leading to more efficient processes and productivity that can be applied across the enterprise.

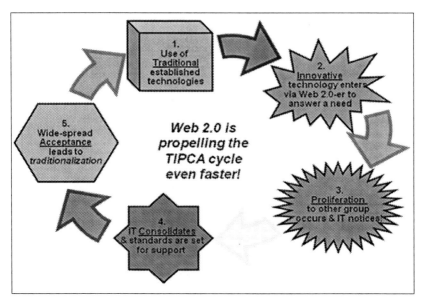

Figure 32: Tradition Innovation Proliferation Consolidation Acceptance (TIPCA) Cycle

Road Map for Collaboration

There are very few organizations today that have reached Stage 5. Most organizations are at stage 2 or 3, and often need help and guidance in moving through these stages to reach higher levels of collaboration and productivity. In fact, many organizations have deployed collaborative tools that far exceed their ability to use them. Because collaborative technologies are the most visible part of the people, process, and technology equation, 80% of the effort typically gets put into the technology segment, which, in reality, is only about 20% of the overall solution. The other 80% that focuses on people and processes generally surfaces in Stages 4 and 5, which are by far the hardest stages to accomplish in the evolutionary process outlined above. Political and cultural elements in the organization can present significant challenges, making it difficult or even impossible to realize the potential benefits of improved collaboration across the enterprise.

Figure 33 shows a ten-step process to help organizations get through Stage 5. It is based on a best practices methodology to achieve success in enterprise collaboration.

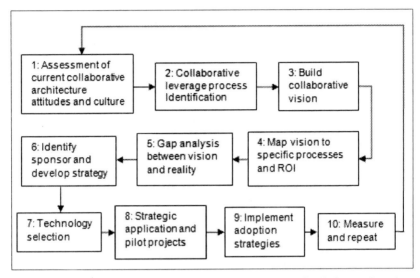

Figure 33: The 10-Step Process to Evolve Collaboration in Your Enterprise

Step 1: Assess Collaborative Environment

The first step in the process is to complete an assessment of the existing collaborative environment (AS IS) in the organization. The assessment should look at the infrastructure and collaborative technologies being used, as well as the culture supporting teaming and collaborative behaviors, and the economic and political impact the application of these technologies is having on the organization. Many organizations go directly to implementing collaboration solutions prior to being ready to adopt and embrace the technology. They don't understand how, where, and when collaboration is actually taking place among the users. IT can often tell you which tools are being used by departments or groups, but they typically cannot tell you the attitudes around collaboration in the organization, or how the organization fosters collaborative and team-oriented behaviors.

The results are predictable. Therefore, it is critical that management and key stakeholders understand the value proposition that improved communication and collaboration can bring to their organization, and where best to apply it before embarking on a project to implement the technology.

The assessment process should identify areas of current or potential collaboration and knowledge sharing across the organization. This information can be obtained from key stakeholders and users of collaborative technologies in the organization, as well as IT, to understand who, what, where, and why questions that provide a comprehensive picture of the AS IS collaborative environment. This information provides a foundation for developing a corporate-wide strategy for the successful deployment of collaboration technologies going forward.

Step 2: Identify Collaborative Business Processes

Collaboration is a behavior, not a technology and there are various communication and coordination technologies that enable collaboration behaviors. When those behaviors occur within critical business processes and are applied appropriately, they can result in significant productivity gains. It is the application of collaborative technology to these processes that are called "collaborative leverage."

The first step is to identify business processes that are highly collaborative. Some common places where collaborative leverage processes reside in every organization include:

- Sales and Marketing (product launches, proposal development, and major account team selling)

- Customer service and support (troubleshooting customer problems)

- R&D (new product development)

- Value network management (relationships with external organizations, distributed project management, and exception handling)

- Training (internal and external)

- Decision support

- Crisis management

This information can be obtained during the interview process in the Assessment step.

Step 3: Build a Collaborative Vision

Prior to implementing collaborative technologies, it is essential to get buy-in and backing from management and key stakeholders in the organization. Without it, collaboration projects stand little chance of succeeding. Education and vision building are effective ways to accomplish this, which can be done through management workshops specifically geared to the organization's industry and key business issues they are trying to address.

A process for doing this can include the following activities:

- An overview of the collaboration market to explain the different kinds of technologies available and how they can be deployed to meet specific needs within an organization.

- Demonstrations using selected collaboration tools help management and key stakeholders envision how the technology can be adopted in their organization.

- Case studies and user stories can also be used.

Demonstrations and case studies should be built around critical business processes identified in Step 2 to show the impact they can have on the organization. The goal of this step is to develop a clear and tangible vision of how people would work, and the benefits that would accrue, if collaborative technologies were implemented successfully across the organization.

Step 4: Build a Business Case for Collaboration

The next step required for gaining management and stakeholder buy-in is to build a business case to justify implementing the collaborative vision at the corporate level. This includes estimating the costs, benefits, and risks associated with implementing the vision it must answer critical business questions such as: "What business problems are we trying to solve?" "What is the business value of a collaboration platform?" and who will fund this initiative?" The business case should outline who, what, when, why, and the how of launching a collaborative initiative, as well as the financial costs and benefits.

Total cost of ownership (TCO) should be used for estimating the costs associated with implementing and supporting an enterprise collaboration platform. These include both direct and indirect costs. Besides TCO, it is important to look at the benefits that would result from using collaboration technologies; these include:

- Decreased cycle times

- Increased productivity

- Increased revenue, profitability, and market share

- Reduced errors and increase quality

- Making better decisions

- Reduced support costs

- Realizing additional benefits from moving these technologies out into the value network

It is also critical to examine potential risks. These can include such things as: the organizational culture does not support collaboration resulting in reduced benefits; increased investment due to required network upgrades; adoption rates of collaborative tools don't meet expectations; and the selected vendor falls behind in technology upgrades.

Completion of this step assumes that management buy-in has been accomplished. If not, more work may need to be done in building the collaborative vision and the business case, which are essential for moving forward with the project.

Step 5: Identify Sponsor

It is common knowledge that a sponsor or champion is behind every successful project. Collaboration projects are no exception. There are always unforeseen challenges that occur and must be resolved to move the project forward. The sponsor should believe in the project fully and the benefits it will bring to the organization. The role of the sponsor is to establish collaboration as a priority and sell the idea and benefits of collaboration to others in the organization. They should also be able to sign off on project budgets and hold teams to specific timelines and milestones.

An executive sponsor should be identified at this step to continue the momentum created so far. They may be a senior manager, experiencing collaborative pain and looking for ways to streamline business processes and improve productivity in their business unit, or someone who has been successful in implementing collaborative technologies in their business unit and can speak to the benefits.

Step 6: Develop a Collaboration Strategy

A strategy for implementing an enterprise collaboration platform should be developed, which supports the vision and the business case. This involves identifying existing collaboration technologies to be consolidated to improve management and control, and reduce risks that may exist from operating in a multi-solution environment. Another activity is developing process maps for the business processes identified in Step 2 that show where collaboration can be leveraged. A trend in the industry is moving toward contextual collaboration, where user access to collaboration features is integrated within the business process or application being used. This can improve rates of adoption, since the use of the collaboration technologies becomes seamlessly melded into the way people work.

Another activity in developing the strategy is determining where gaps exist between the existing AS IS collaborative environment and the TO BE collaborative vision environment, and how to fix them. Examples where gaps may exist include:

- The current infrastructure may need to be upgraded to support the proposed collaborative environment. Insufficient bandwidth is a common problem in organizations looking to implement high bandwidth solutions like video conferencing across a distributed enterprise.

- Existing security models and policies may need to be strengthened to adequately support the TO BE environment. Moving from an environment where IM policies don't exist, and various public IM systems are in use, to an enterprise IM environment requires policy and security decisions to be implemented.

- New types of collaborative software may need to be implemented that require user training across the enterprise. Implementing Web/video conferencing solutions in organizations where they have had limited use requires user training and education on where and when to use them effectively.

- Existing processes may need to be streamlined to take full advantage of the new collaboration solutions. This may involve changing workflow and employee job responsibilities.

The strategy should recommend a prioritized list of collaboration programs (initiatives) that deliver value to the organization. Note it may be prudent to only launch one or two programs at a time due to the resources required to properly manage and implement the program.

Project managers should be assigned to head-up each program from this point forward. They are responsible for the coordination of tasks and resources to execute the collaborative strategy. The project manager also keeps management informed of progress and seeks help from management when difficult challenges arise that require senior level decisions and support.

Step 7: Select Collaboration Technology

This is a tactical step that involves selecting the vendor that best meets the overall requirements for the proposed collaboration program. Because the collaborative technology market has a large number of players and is very competitive, there are potentially a number of qualified vendors that provide solutions for the proposed program. A short list of vendors should be created based on a preliminary investigation of possible candidates. A formal RFP process may be used to obtain proposals from the short list of vendors or a more direct approach involving detailed briefings and demonstrations can be employed to evaluate each vendor solution.

The evaluation process should address product requirements based on specific application features, which vary by solution type, as well as generic requirements such as:

- Security
- Reliability
- Scalability
- Ability to customize
- Ease of use
- Integration with other applications
- User operating environments
- Product roadmap
- Total Cost of Ownership

Vendor requirements should address criteria including the financial viability of the company, the company's customer base, their training and support organization, etc.

As a final part of the vendor selection process, the evaluation team should prepare a ROI analysis for the recommended solution. This validates the business case for management based on actual costs and provides them with renewed assurances an investment in the collaboration technology will pay off.

Step 8: Pilot Project

After selecting the collaborative solution, a pilot project should be initiated to validate the capabilities of the recommended solution before rolling it out to the rest of the organization. The business unit selected for the pilot should meet a set of predefined criteria that make it a good candidate for testing the capabilities of the solution against the requirements. Prior to launching the pilot project, planning should cover issues such as user training, user support, metrics for measuring the program, program monitoring, and management reporting. The pilot should be monitored closely. If problems arise, they should be resolved quickly.

Note that it is important to make the pilot program successful. Results of the pilot can be used as a positive marketing tool to build awareness and interest in the rest of the organization. Pilot programs also serve to develop the best ways to roll out the solution to other parts of the organization and achieve high adoption rates.

A word about SaaS: A major IT market research firm says that in 2007, 25% of all software is offered as a service and by 2012, 50% of all software will be offered this way. There are some clear advantages to the SaaS model:

- You don't need in-house hardware or expertise.

- The service is often free to try and you can buy if it works for you.

- These services, because the environment is so competitive, often require no or little training to get up to speed and running on the application.

- Initial costs are much lower.

- There are no versions, maintenance, or upgrades with a service as there are with licensed software.

Many of our clients are taking advantage of the SaaS revolution and, with the blessing of IT, are doing their pilot projects this way with less cost and less risk.

Step 9: Enterprise Rollout

The pilot project serves as a precursor to rolling out the collaborative solution to the rest of the organization. What is learned in the pilot can be applied to the general rollout. Careful planning and execution is a must to insure success.

- Prioritize the business units for implementation.

- Identify the required resources to support the rollout.

- Define the process for delivering education and training to management and users.

- Define the process for resolving issues that arise.

- Define the metrics for measuring adoption rates among the users.

CS has looked at organizations adopting collaborative tools for over a decade. A variety of end-user organizations and vendors were interviewed in 2004-2005 regarding critical success factors for collaboration technologies. Table 13 shows the results of these interviews. The left column shows these factors from the end user's point of view, and the right column shows what the situation looks like from the vendor's point of view.

Table 13:   Critical Success Factors and the Potential Impact on Adoption

End User Critical Success Factors	Vendor's View of Adoption Challenges
Collaboration technology projects need to be tied to specific and important business needs felt by the actual users of the technology.	The technology is only being used by a small part of the organization, and has stalled in terms of proliferating to the rest of the organization.
The adoption project needs to be led by a single influential champion and have the active support of key executives.	The vendor has identified a need, but either the end-user does not see it as a collaboration problem or there is no influential champion for the technology.

End User Critical Success Factors	Vendor's View of Adoption Challenges
Clear business processes exist, are well defined, and are compatible with the technology.	Technology was purchased by IT and is now in search of an appropriate business process or problem in the organization to justify it.
There needs to be clear and meaningful metrics to measure success.	Usage is growing, but key decision-makers are not convinced of the effectiveness of the technology.
It is easy to learn how to use the new technology through: – Excellent up-front training and support. – Technology that is inherently easy to use. – Active involvement and support by IT. – Small projects that take on more as competence with the technology grows.	Although tied to a clear business need and metrics showing success where it is used, people who otherwise would use it are instead claiming they don't have time to learn how.
After a successful pilot, end users effectively build upon and advertise their success to other groups.	A successful pilot should be followed by an increase in seat sales, but the end-user does not know how to do a successful deployment of collaboration technologies.
User deployment plan places significant emphasis on addressing people and cultural issues.	IT has a deployment plan and has already run into stiff resistance. Their plan only takes into account technical issues and has a low chance of success.

It was clear from the interviews that both vendors and end-user organizations under-estimated the complexity of the adoption problem for collaborative technologies. Both groups were aware of the cultural/behavioral impact these technologies could have. However, very few interviewees in either group knew how to deal with these issues successfully to help drive adoption. Some of the most common issues observed included the following:

- The end user organization struggled with collaboration technologies when there was a clear business need for collaboration, but there was no champion to drive adoption through the organization.

- The end user organization was having problems generating an urgent need for introducing collaborative technology throughout the organization.

- The adoption rate for the end-user organization had dropped and it wasn't immediately clear what was causing the problem. Note that it is possible for organizations to have a clear champion, clear business reasons for implementing the technology, a clear ROI, a single focused solution, a clear technical plan, and still run into organizational resistance. Resistance to change by the people can surface as the hardest issue to overcome in adopting collaborative technologies.

A number of sub-issues were also identified in the survey. They are characterized in the following quotes from people who were interviewed in the survey:

- *"People are used to doing things in person, people are used to picking up the phone, so they just go back to doing things the way they used to."*

- *"Some companies want to travel and wine and dine. It is a company cultural thing and negates the major benefits of collaborative technology."*

- *"We are changing the culture in the way they are going about doing their business. It is hard to get a subset of people to change their behavior."*

- *"We have a cultural norm of people wanting to physically attend meetings that are in the same physical location."*

- *"There is a perception that web conferencing is for special events only."*

- *"We started having problems in our business revenue and the resistance grew out of a sense that people didn't have time to change, just get busy going after more revenue."*

- *"If there is something that has worked for them in the past it is very hard to get people to stop using it."*

Step 10: Measure and Report

Measuring and reporting on the adoption and usage of collaborative technologies during and after the enterprise rollout is completed is critical to the on-going success of the program and reaching Stage 5–Virtual Work Environment. Being vigilant in monitoring and assessing how the collaborative technologies are being used leads to increased usage productivity, as well as meeting the goals outlined in the business case.

Coleman's Law

"People resist change, and organizations resist change to an exponentially greater degree!"

A corollary to this law is: *"The larger the organization, the greater the change, or the more complex the project, the greater the exponent for the resistance to change."*

This resistance is true for any technology that supports some kind of social interaction. Resistance is usually a fact with any new technology or a significant change in business process. One of the most interesting things we saw over-and-over was what happened when IT brought collaboration technologies into the organization. Typically, IT did a very thorough evaluation of the technology and how it would fit with the current infrastructure. However, most technology organizations did not look at the people and process issues that these collaboration technologies would cause.

When we explained to them that introducing collaboration technologies changes the way people communicate and interact with each other, and this in turn changes the corporate structure. The response we usually get from IT was something like "What do you mean it changes the corporate structure?" accompanied by a "deer in the headlights" look on their face. Most IT people have no knowledge of corporate structures and interpersonal interactions; after all, that is the realm of the HR people. Just getting HR and IT people to talk about the problem together was often a difficult task. Although both groups were speaking English, because they had very little context in common, it often required me to act as a translator between the two groups putting what each said into a context and terminology the other could understand.

Recommendations for Success

Based on these and other experiences of collaboration in the enterprise, the following recommendations are applicable to the integration of any new program or process to facilitate the use of collaboration technologies:

- **Apply the new tool initially where there is a clear opportunity to achieve ROI quickly.** Leverage the momentum of the initial success to extend the application to more and more difficult challenges.

- **Integrate the tool into critical business processes.** Busy professionals do not want to take the time to learn a new software tool if it is not going to specifically address their needs, be readily adopted by others, and not too difficult or time-consuming to learn.

- **Assure smooth integration with existing dependent process applications and work flow.** A new application must be able to integrate into the current work setting. Therefore, it must work with or not inhibit the use of other applications currently in use. Additionally, it must mirror (as best as possible) the current workflow and be flexible to adjust to changes.

- **Develop best practices** to demonstrate the value of collaboration technologies across the enterprise.

- **Find a "champion" who will promote the use of collaboration technologies** throughout the enterprise and has the authority to recognize and reward individuals for their contribution to collaborative work.

- **Plan for and address change management issues** that may arise during the deployment of collaboration technologies throughout the enterprise.

- **Develop and implement appropriate security models** that protect internal intellectual property while still allowing for and promoting communication openness. These models may need to be adjusted as team needs change.

Let us assume that your organization, like many others in the US, is at stage 2 or 3 and is looking for other collaboration tools to help with the changing business environment seen in today's Web 2.0 world. The following questions can help determine whether a team requires a VTS tool and if so, what functionality and features to look for when making the choice:

- Do you regularly work with people outside your organization across time and space? Other centers, external partners (industry, academia, etc.)?

- How large is the group you work in?

- Do your team members utilize various computer platforms, operating systems, and browsers?

- Are you finding it hard to manage your team's information and productivity?

- Are e-mail and other communication tools used by your team creating information silos, resulting in lost knowledge, security issues, and duplication of effort?

- Does your team create frequent deliverables/documents that must be reviewed, edited, and version-controlled?

- Do you have projects with meeting notes, schedules, and tasks/subtasks that must be tracked, reported, and summarized?

- Does your team have business processes that require approvals, threaded discussions, and team calendars?

- Do you have a current collaboration tool initiative in place? If so, what are you currently using and how well does it serve your needs?

- Are you facing issues with end-user adoption, user interface, features, or performance?

- Would you and your team benefit from a system that allows you to centrally store and track documents, provide version control and search, conduct and archive electronic communication (synchronously and asynchronously) all in an accessible, secure location?

- Are there other teams in your organization that are facing similar challenges? If so, what have they done?

- What approaches are you taking to build trust among distributed team members?

- How do you drive consensus in a virtual team space?

- How do you establish and communicate priorities in a virtual team space?

- What is the ratio of people working together and independently in a virtual team space?

- How critical is security; how critical is access?

In reviewing your answers to these questions, consider the top priorities for your team, and use these to filter all the various application options available to you. You do not want to get into the trap of selecting an application based on a litany of feature bells and whistles that your team is not likely to use. Rather, concentrate on significant aspects of your team's workflow, current trust level, technical savvy and the top four or five features or functions that your team will be using. This will help narrow the field when you go searching for the right application for your team.

16 Collaboration and the World View

> "Most of man's problems in the modern world arise from the constant and unavoidable exposure to the stimuli of urban and industrial civilization, the varied aspects of environmental pollution, the physiological disturbances associated with sudden changes in ways of life, the estrangement from the conditions and natural cycles under which human evolution took place, the emotional trauma and the paradoxical solitude in congested cities, the monotony, boredom and compulsory leisure—in brief, all the environmental conditions that undisciplined technology creates."
> —René Jules Dubos, *So Human an Animal*

The World is Flat, and absent a complete breakdown in transportation and technology, it is not going back. Given how economies, organizations, and people are working together, it is essential to collaborate virtually. That said, the benefits of Collaboration 2.0 include:

- Ability to work across borders

- Ability to work with the best people no matter where they are located

- Reduced travel costs

- Reduced human costs

- Reduced environmental costs

- Greater efficiency in the production process

In order to work in the space effectively, People, Process, and Technology must all be addressed simultaneously. Excluding any one of these critical elements will result in failure. Some people think all they need is great technology that incorporates a great process. Unfortunately, that will not do it.

If you want to be successful in the world of Collaboration 2.0, it will be essential to communicate to the people on the other side of the technology and process, that human skill and capacity is the glue that holds it all together.

This book is a lot to absorb. Effective collaboration is not always very easy, and when it looks easy it probably took a lot of effort and planning. Many chapters had to be taken out including: a chapter on Mashups and Collaboration; the role of attention in collaboration; generational preferences for collaboration tools; various case studies; collaborative assessment tools, etc.

Much of this material will go into the online community that is being developed around Collaboration 2.0. We believe that books are static and that people are dynamic, and so we are looking for a way to make this book more dynamic. One of the ways to do this is to publish the book in an online community in a wiki format, so that those who read it can ask questions make comments and generally make the book a living and hopefully more collaborative document. If you want to join this community, please see: http://collaborate.com/book.

World View of Collaboration

In this book we have talked a lot about collaboration and how it affects the individual, the team, group, department, enterprise, but not how it affects society and the world as a whole. We thought it appropriate to end the book with this worldview and look at how collaboration affects each and every one of us through environmental sustainability.

Conclusion: Collaboration and Sustainability

We recently attended a semi-annual symposium put on by NewWoW, which is the brain child of Joe Ouye and Jim Creighton, is essentially composed of three groups of people: HR people, technology people, and real estate/facilities people. It's really an interesting mix of experts, and the symposium this time was on sustainability, and to see if new ways of working, that is working from home, a satellite office, working in distributed teams across geographies and so forth would help with sustainability.

But what is sustainability? As anyone who has seen now Nobel Peace Prize recipient Al Gore's *"An Inconvenient Truth"* (Stewart was trained to deliver the slide show by Al and will do it for you pro bono)[41] knows the polar ice caps are melting and the level of CO_2 in the air is 100 parts/million higher than it was 100 years ago.

There are some companies (IBM, HP, Sun, Google, etc.) that are doing a lot to be sustainable or "green" through solar power, bussing employees, and a variety of other methods to cut down their carbon footprint. But the fact is that the growing population in China has great power demands, and that 544 new coal burning power plants will be coming on line worldwide over the next few years (coal power plants are one of the dirtiest ways of producing power and coal-fired generators emit roughly twice the national average for emissions) means that all we do to cut our carbon footprint is more than negated by the new power plants coming on line.

I (David) found this message rather depressing; after all I work from home to try to reduce my commuting to Silicon Valley. I have cut my air travel (which by the way is one of the worst offenders in terms of introducing CO_2 into the upper atmosphere where it has 3X more effect on global warming) from over 100,000 miles a year, to less than 20,000. But "no good deed goes unpunished" and the result of reducing my carbon footprint is that, when I do fly, I get the worst seats on the plane every time (stuck in the middle next to a crying baby), and all of it may have no effect on environmental sustainability.

---

41. Albert Gore, *An Inconvenient Truth*, (New York: Rodale, 2006).

According to experts, that does not mean we should not do everything possible to lower our carbon footprint. The environmental impact by 2050 will be more than 4x what it was in 2000 and by the end of the 21st century it is projected to be 11.6 times greater than it was at the beginning of the century. If we look at how much the U.S. participates in this global warming, we have a population of 300 million (5% of the world population) and yet we use 25% of the world's energy. According to the Stern Review Final Report, transportation industry uses (14%) and the power industries (25%), and they are the two biggest culprits contributing to global warming. However, there is hope! GreatPoint Energy is commercializing a technology to convert coal to natural gas—turning one of the dirtiest fuels into one of the cleanest.

Your Collaborative Carbon Footprint

We know that web and video conferencing have cut down personally on our travel. But is there an easy way to determine if using any collaborative technologies is making our carbon footprint smaller or larger?

Recently there were some answers and positive outcomes around collaboration and sustainability. One web conferencing company has come up not only with a carbon footprint calculator, but with a whole sustainability program.

iLinc Communications, Inc., a developer of Web and audio conferencing software announced that customers, partners, and employees participating in its iReduce program have saved a combined total of one billion pounds of CO_2 from January to September (2007) by choosing Web and audio conferencing instead of travel. All iLinc customers can easily measure their CO_2 savings by viewing the company's carbon calculator and even tracking their progress on their iLinc account management page. In addition, for every iLinc customer that saves a million pounds or more of CO_2 every quarter, the company will donate money in the customer's name toward renewable energy sources and carbon reduction efforts.

The iLinc Web conferencing software automatically calculates exactly how much CO_2 emissions are saved for every individual that uses the iLinc product through a patent-pending feature called the iLinc Green Meter™. By detecting the locations of the people that are attending the

Web meeting and measuring the distance between the meeting participants and the meeting leader, the iLinc Green Meter can measure the exact amount of travel that is eliminated. The Meter then applies an algorithm that recognizes what means of travel would commonly be used for the distance (such as car, small aircraft, large aircraft, etc.) and generates a CO_2 emissions savings amount for both the Web meeting leader and a composite number for their entire organization. I recently talked with Avistar (a video conferencing vendor) who also indicated they were in the process of building a carbon footprint calculator.

From my experience (Stewart) educating myself over the past few years and presenting the "Inconvenient Truth" slideshow, there is a great deal of hope, but we need to act quickly and remember every bit counts. Small things like changing light bulbs, insulating homes, solar energy, turning up/down thermostats, how and what we drive...it all adds up. The recent annual conference of The Association for the Advancement of Science ended with a few key presentations on what we can do. What was interesting was that the day after the conference venture capital people were meeting with members of the scientific community looking for ideas to fund. I am familiar with an executive search firm that has a green division. For more things you can do, check out The Rocky Mountain Institute at http://www.rmi.org and *The Low Carbon Diet* by David Gershon.[42]

All this positive activity leads us to believe that advancements in technology got us into this mess, and they may be able to get us out. However, the solution again comes down to people and process, with the technology as an "enabler." If we can all get over some of our differences and pull together, it seems possible to reduce or remove the destruction we have caused the earth and our environment. One of the benefits of collaboration technologies (aside from less air travel) is that it brings people in disparate geographies together, and can make us feel part of the larger "human" family. And perhaps the connections we make all over the globe will foster diverse distributed educational conversations that will wake us up to how precious life on this planet is.

---

42. David Gershon, *The Low Carbon Diet,* (Woodstock: Empowerment Institute, 2006).

Resources for
Collaboration in a
Web 2.0 World

AdaptiveBlue.com: A Smart Browsing and Personalization Company

Uses products like BlueOrganizer, which recognizes content and retrieves related information from other sites.

http://www.adaptiveblue.com

Adobe Systems Incorporated

Creator of consumer and professional mobile, print, photography, and web tools. Products include Acrobat Connect (formerly Macromedia's Breeze), the Acrobat family, After Effects, ColdFusion, Dreamweaver, Flash, InDesign, and more.

http://www.adobe.com

Akiva Corporation

Provides open collaboration solutions to fit any enterprise collaboration environment. Products include Silk (an open source collaboration platform; www.silk-project.org), WebBoard (a web-based discussion tool for Windows servers), and ChatSpace.

http://www.akiva.com

Altexa

An offsite internet data backup software provider, Altexa Backup.

http://www.altexa.com

Altus Learning Systems

Provides post-production on video and supports transcription and video indexing down to the word.

http://www.altuslearning.com

Amazon.com, Inc.

Provides hosting services called Elastic Compute Cloud (EC2) virtual hosting service and the Amazon Simple Storage Service (S3)

http://www.amazon.com

AMI Consortium

Envisions individual and group activities between and during meetings, dramatically enhancing business productivity with the use of advanced signal processing and knowledge management. User interface called JFerret as well as Distributed Virtual Meeting, Meeting Archive Browsing, and the Mobile Meeting Capture System.

http://www.ami-project.com

Apple Inc.

iTunes, creative software, action and family games, Pro Design, and productivity tools.

http://www.apple.com

Areae, Inc.

Developer of a virtual world that easily integrates.

http://www.areae.net

Atlassian Software Systems Pty Ltd

A global software company providing enterprise software such as confluence, a wiki provider.

http://www.atlassian.com

Autodesk, Inc.

A leader in 2-D and 3-D design, project collaboration software tools, and digital content creation including AutoCad, Constructware, and AutoSketch.

http://usa.autodesk.com

Avistar Communications Corporation

Provider of enterprise video communications solutions.

http://www.avistar.com

Bay Partners

Partners with entrepreneurs in information technology and health care businesses, providing SaaS.

http://www.baypartners.com

BEA Systems, Inc.

Design infrastructure software to transform business; products include BEA AquaLogic, BEA WebLogic, and BEA Tuxedo. BEA Systems also owns PlumTree, a software company.

http://www.bea.com

Berrett-Koehler Publishers

Independent publishers of books that advance social responsibility in business and the individual.

http://www.bkconnection.com

Blizzard Entertainment

Creator of gaming universes such as Warcraft, Diablo, and StarCraft.

http://www.blizzard.com

Blockbuster Inc.

A video and DVD online and brick-and-mortar superstores.

http://www.blockbuster.com

Blue Marble Geographics

A geographic software tool company and developer of GIS developer components.

http://www.bluemarblegeo.com

BoonEx Ltd

Flexible and powerful community software and implement ideas in real life. Product line includes Dolphin 6, Ray 3, and BoonEx ID.

http://www.boonex.com

Calgoo Software

A Java-based application that syncs online and offline calendars. Partners with Google and Microsoft.

http://www.calgoo.com

Central Desktop, Inc.

Provides simple project collaboration tools for business teams to efficiently organize and share information and collaborate on projects.

http://www.centraldesktop.com

CEO Space

A leader in online collaboration.

http://www.ceospace.biz

Charles River Quick Start program

A venture fund that offers small amounts of capital for "getting good ideas started."

http://www.crv.com

Cisco Systems, Inc

A leading supplier of networking equipment and management for the internet, with products including WebEx WebOffice, and the Unified Communications System.

http://www.cisco.com

Clarizen Inc.

Collaborative project management for businesses.

http://www.clarizen.com

CNET Networks, Inc.

A destination for tech product reviews, tech news, daily videos, podcasts, and ZDNet's software directory, which covers software for Windows, Mac, and Mobile systems.

http://www.cnet.com

CoCreate Software, Inc.

Provider of collaborative software for engineering product design including the OneSpace suite supporting product development and lifecycle management.

http://www.cocreate.com

CollabNet, Inc.

A collaborative platform for multi-site software development.

http://www.collab.net

Collaborative Strategies

Advises vendors marketing collaborative solutions and end-user companies interested in implementing such collaborative solutions. Home of the Collaboration Blog.

http://www.collaborate.com

Collanos Software AG

Workplace software allows for sharing of documents, online discussions, and management of tasks within a single space.

http://www.collanos.com

CommunityXperts

A compilation of the best information and latest information on Web 2.0, online communities, and offers best practices and consulting in implementing those communities.

http://www.communityxperts.com

Comverse Technology, Inc.

New avatar service called Klonies for mobile services. (Not yet available in the U.S.)

http://www.comverse.com

Craigslist

A community moderated forum of local classifieds and forums for 450 cities worldwide.

http://www.craigslist.org

Donnewood Media

Meez allows the creation of a caricature of oneself to be used anywhere.

http://www.meez.com.

eBay

A worldwide auction site of goods posted and monitored by the consumer. eBay also has acquired Skype, PayPal, and invests in Craigslist.

http://www.ebay.com

Eclipse Foundation

Open source community of projects focused on building an open development platform comprised of extensible frameworks, tools, and runtimes for building and managing software across the lifecycle.

http://www.eclipse.org

Element Software

The Copper project, project management tool and software helps teams collaborate and manage themselves more effectively.

http://www.copperproject.com

ElephantDrive, Inc.

Provides unlimited online storage for all file types.

http://www.elephantdrive.com

EMC Documentum

The eRoom product enables enterprises to become more productive by bringing together people, content, and processes to optimize projects.

http://www.documentum.com

eProject Inc.

Offers project management software and tools for resource planning and project portfolio management.

http://www.eproject.com

Geezeo

A social finance application that assists in the making of educated financial decisions.

http://www.geezeo.com

Glance Networks, Inc.

Desktop sharing for web demos, presentations, and webinars.

http://www.glance.net

Google

Began as a search engine, now includes server-side integration with AOL and ICQ. Now includes GoogleTalk, and telephone service/access to high-speed internet as well as JotSpot (http://www.jot.com), YouTube (http://www.youtube.com), Deja, Outride, Pyra, Applied Semantics, Kaltix, Sprinks, Ignite Logic, Neotonic, Picasa, Writley, and Keyhole. Invests in Ubiquisys.

http://www.google.com

GreatPoint Energy Inc.

A domestic energy company that is seeking to reduce the U.S. dependence on imported natural gas.

http://www.greatpointenergy.com

Grove Technologies

Online collaboration workspaces that are simple like a wiki, but designed for businesses.

http://www.grovesite.com

Happy About

Publisher of quick to read, high-impact books for business and the consumer, including positive impact stories and management books.

http://www.happyabout.info

HeartMath LLC

Combines leading edge science, practical information, and easily used techniques and skills for achieving well-being and reducing stress.

http://www.Heartmath.com

Herman Miller Inc

A global provider of office furniture and services to create spaces in which to live, learn, work, and heal.

http://www.hermanmiller.com

Hewlett Packard

Leading producer of computer apparatus, including printers, cameras, servers, storage and networking solutions, and software, as well as laptops and desktop computers.

http://www.hp.com

HTC Corporation

Recently released the Advantage X7501 PocketPC using Windows Mobile 6. Also provides the iMate Jasjar (a universal 3G phone).

http://www.htc.com

huddle

A network of secure online spaces that combine powerful project, team, and document tools that is as simple to operate as a social networking site.

http://www.huddle.net

IBM

Lotus Notes, Lotus Domino, Quickplace, Workplace, SameTime WebDialogs (web conferencing, including Unyte), FileNet, and Watchfire. Software utilizing IBM tools includes the Firefox web browser, OASIS open document format, and the WebSphere portal v6 on Red Hat Desktop Linux or Novel SUSE Desktop Linux suites.

http://www.ibm.com

iLinc Communications, Inc.

A provider of web conferencing software and audio conferencing solutions.

http://www.ilinc.com

IMVU

A 3-D avatar chat and instant messenger dress up game.

http://www.imvu.com

Inter-Tel

Web conferencing and remote support software solutions that provide real-time communications and support for help desks via the internet.

http://www.linktivity.com

Interwise, Inc. (now AT&T)

Voice, web, and video conferencing for businesses using Interwise Connect.

http://www.interwise.com

iPolipo, Inc.

Helps professionals schedule meetings automatically by selectively and securely sharing your calendar with those you need to meet.

http://www.ipolipo.com

Jaxtr, Inc

A service that links your telephone to the Web, allowing for private calls worldwide.

http://www.jaxtr.com

JetArk Holdings, Inc.

A browser companion that creates and holds "jetpaks" of information dragged and dropped from anywhere on the web.

http://www.jeteye.com

Jive Software

Collaboration software that is highly configurable and extensive. Includes Clearspace, ClearspaceX, and Openfire.

http://www.jivesoftware.com

Jungle Tools LLC

An application called Jungle Disk that allows for the storage of files and backup data securely to Amazon.com's S3.

http://www.jungledisk.com

Kazaa

Provides peer-to-peer availability of songs at a manageable price.

http://www.kazaa.com

Knexa Solutions Ltd.

Provides web-based collaboration, knowledge exchange software, virtual teamwork, and online project management.

http://www.knexa.com

Knowledge Ability Ltd

Training and consulting in virtual teaming, collaboration tools, and remote work abilities.

http://www.knowab.co.uk

Kwiki

A wiki engine designed for easy installation and modularity.

http://www.kwiki.org

LinkedIn Corporation

A networking tool that strengthens and extends an existing network of trusted contacts.

http://www.linkedin.com

LiteScape Technologies, Inc.

Product allows integration of sources including LDAP, Active Directory, Yahoo, AOL, Outlook, Sametime, CUCS, and mobile devices.

http://www.litescape.com

MediaWiki Introduction

A free software wiki package, used by the Wikimedia Foundation and Wikipedia.

http://www.mediawiki.org

MeetingSense Software Corporation

Offers solutions for meeting productivity.

http://www.meetingsense.com

Microsoft Corporation

LiveMeeting with Arel Anywhere (video conferencing), SharePoint services, Exchange, Office Collaboration Suite. Groove Networks functionality built into Vista. The Unified Communications Group. Office, Windows, Internet Explorer, PocketPC.

http://www.microsoft.com

Motley Fool

A financial education company with the motto "to educate, enrich, and amuse individual investors around the world." Includes a discussion board on retirement investment is good example of open forum for feedback on a wide variety of vendor sites.

Mozilla

Developer of Firefox, a Web browser that is fast, secure, and fully customizable.

http://www.firefox.com

Multiverse Network, Inc

Creates a platform for 3-D virtual worlds and allows avatars to move from one world to the next.

http://www.multiverse.net

Near-Time, Inc.

Integrates wikis, blogs, and file-sharing to deliver the fastest return on collaboration investments. Hosts http://collaborate.com/book/.

http://www.near-time.net

NetAge, Inc.

Collaboration, virtual teams, teamnets, and networks with virtual tools. Wrote the Forward of this book.

http://www.netage.com

Netflix

Online DVD rental company.

http://www.netflix.com

New Ways of Working

A membership organization that brings together thought leaders to discuss new ways of working in a distributed world.

http://www.NewWoW.net

Nexo Systems, Inc.

Provides free websites and email lists to allow groups to collaborate online.

http://www.nexo.com

Novell, Inc.

Offers enterprise infrastructure software and services including Hula (an Open Source collaboration tool).

http://www.novell.com

Oddcast Inc.

Authoring tool that allows for users to create and embed customized animated characters, including Voki (http://www.voki.com).

http://www.oddcast.com

Open Text Corporation

Moved itself out of the collaboration market to focus on document and content management.

http://www.opentext.com

Openfount

Utilizes Amazon S3 storage and the Google Web Toolkit to allow a solo developer to deploy an AJAX application to the Web.

http://www.openfount.com

OpenSAM

An Office-like integration framework.

http://www.opensam.org

OpenTeams LLC

Web-hosted collaborative software for entrepreneurs.

http://www.openteams.com

Open-Xchange Inc.

Scalable and integrated open source email and collaboration solutions.

http://www.open-xchange.com

Options for Change

An organizational development learning group and consulting practice.

http://www.optionsforchange.com

Oracle

Collaboration Suite with Virtual Team Rooms, own PeopleSoft and Siebel Systems.

http://www.oracle.com

Persony

Able to provide video conferencing via Flash 7 mobile.

http://www.persony.com

PhpBB Group

An Open Source forum solution with easy-to-use administration panel and user-friendly installation process.

http://www.phpbb.com

phpGroupWare

PhpGroupWare is a web-based multi-user groupware suite with over 50 applications that can be mixed and matched to meet the user's needs.

http://www.phpgroupware.org

Planview

Partners with the world's leading organizations to address the need for innovation in a resource-challenged business climate.

http://www.Planview.com

Plaxo, Inc.

A free service that securely updates and maintains the information in your address book.

http://www.plaxo.com

Pmwiki

A wiki-based system for the creation and maintenance of web sites in a collaborative manner.

http://www.pmwiki.org

Projity Incorporated

Provides software as a service project management solutions and desktop project management software.

http://www.openproj.org

Q2Learning LLC

Builds software for knowledge-intensive organizations, providing collaboration tools for the creation of results-based learning and knowledge sharing.

http://www.q2learning.com

Quick2Publish

Writes and publishes books for corporations that are interested in establishing thought leadership and generating leads, but don't have the time to write themselves.

http://www.quick2publish.com

Qwaq, Inc.

Makes, sells, and supports secure interactive persistent virtual workspaces.

http://www.qwaq.com

Saba

People management tools including Centra, Talent, and the Performance Suite.

http://www.saba.com

salesforce.com, inc.

Provides customer relationship management software services to assist companies with global customer communication. Products include the AppExchange, Successforce, and salesforce.

http://www.salesforce.com

Second Life

A resident-created 3-D virtual world.

http://www.secondlife.com

ShareMethods

Provides centralized and secure document creation and sharing.

http://www.ShareMethods.com

Sierra Adoption Services

An adoption agency in California.

http://www.sierraadoption.org

SiteScape

A VTS vendor with gadgets/widgets that display useful info such as email or weather updates; created a portlet economy, allowing third party developers to market integrateable portlets and share the sale.

http://www.sitescape.com

Skire, Inc.

Drag and Drop tools for project management.

http://www.skire.com

SmugMug, Inc.

Online photo sharing, easy-to-create online photo albums, and tools to share, store, organize, and print photos.

http://www.smugmug.com

SocialText

An enterprise wiki provider for the business world.

http://www.socialtext.com

Sophia's Garden Foundation

A non-profit that works with families with kids that have terminal illnesses. One project is HICO that is trying to help move online communities to support these families online.

http://www.sophiasgarden.org

SQBox Solutions, Ltd

An all-in-one intranet software program with content management and formatting built in.

http://www.Intranetconnections.com

SRI Consulting Business Intelligence

An international technology, consumer research, business, industry, and consulting company.

http://www.sric-bc.com

Sun Microsystems Laboratories

Software research and development company. Products include Sun Ray, Solaris, and Java.

http://www.sun.com

Synchris, Inc.

A provider of virtual workspace software that integrates workflow, document management, communication, and collaboration features. Includes Privia, software to improve task order response and management.

http://www.synchris.com

Tacit Software, Inc

Collaboration software that enables employees to connect others and leverage the collective knowledge of their organization, including illumio and ActiveNet.

http://www.tacit.com

TechCrunch

A group-edited blog about the Web 2.0 sector and other technology startups.

http://www.techcrunch.com

Technorati, Inc.

Provides popularity indexes and real-time search for user-generated media.

http://www.technorati.com

The Frontline Group

A consulting group with a legacy of organizational learning and knowledge management.

http://www.frontline-group.com

The Rocky Mountain Institute

Change how people approach design to help them maximize efficiency.

http://www.rmi.org

TimeBridge, Inc.

Makes the negotiation for a meeting time more efficient and allows for shared information re: the meeting to be disseminated easily.

http://www.timebridge.com

Trichys

The TeamWorkZone product brings external and internal project teams together for collaboration, task assignment, and document sharing.

http://www.teamworkzone.com

Tungle Corporation

Uses peer-to-peer communications to coordinate meetings and integrates with Outlook, Lotus Notes, and Google Calendar; allows users to maintain current calendar in any of the above programs.

http://www.tungle.com

Twiki

Enterprise wiki software, enterprise collaboration, and knowledge management system.

http://www.twiki.org

UbiquiSys Limited

Creates base stations intended to boost wireless coverage insides homes and buildings.

http://www.ubiquisys.com

Vignette Corporation

Provides software to assist organizations in improving the way they interact online with their key audiences; includes Vignette Collaboration, which helps create workspaces that extend current productivity tools.

http://www.vignette.com

Viodia

A test engineering company specializing in test management and automatic test applications to support complex manufacturing companies.

http://www.viodia.com

Virtual Worlds News

An online source for virtual worlds business news, insight, analysis, and strategy.

http://www.virtualworldsnews.com

Volutio

New product called ikordo (formerly Meeting Agent), which schedules meetings via email communications. Has a plug in allowing for integration with Microsoft Outlook.

http://www.volutio.com

WebDialogs, Inc.

Provides voice and web conferencing solutions for business. Acquired by IBM.

http://www.webdialogs.com

WebEx Communications

Online web collaboration software for online meetings, conferencing, and desktop sharing. Acquired by Cisco.

http://www.webex.com

Webmail.us, Inc

An email hosting company.

http://www.webmail.us

Wikipedia

A free-content encyclopedia using wiki software and completely editable by users.

http://www.wikipedia.com

WikiWikiWeb

An online database editable by every member.

http://www.Wikiwikiweb.com

WuFoo

An online HTML form builder for forms, surveys, and invitations.

http://www.wufoo.com

Yahoo, Inc.

An online community, news, and communication network. Includes Zimbra ("Zimlets" or widgets), bought eGroups, and Flickr.com, an online photo sharing and management application.

http://www.yahoo.com

YouTube

User-uploaded videos for general viewing, sharing, and storage.

http://www.youtube.com

Zimbra

Open source email and calendar groupware software. Acquired by Yahoo!

http://www.zimbra.com

Other Resources and Tools

Virtual Worlds

Doppleganger; Kaneva; Meez, Active Worlds; Coke Studios; Club Penguin; Cybertown; Disney's Toontown; Dreamville; Dubit; Habbo Hotel; The Manor; Mokitown; Moove; Muse; The Palace; Playdo; The Sims Online; Sora City; There; TowerChat; Traveler; Virtual Ibiza; Virtual Magic Kingdom; Voodoo Chat; VPchat; VZones; whyrobbierocks; Whyville; Worlds.com; Yohoho! Puzzle Pirates; Gaia Online

Social Network and Community Tools

Q2Learning, iCohere, Affinity Circles, GroupMembersOnly, Google Groups, Yahoo Groups, Collanos, Foldera, Leverage Software, Smallworldlabs, Social Platform, Web Crossing, CollectiveX, Me.com, Sparta Social Networks, Friendster, Facebook, MySpace, Tribe

Additional Resources

We are offering a workshop based on the principles, processes and technologies found in this book. We have an outline for the workshop below:

Collaboration 2.0

Developing High-Performance and Sustainable Collaboration within Virtual Teams

One Day Workshop

Note: This is a hands-on workshop; everyone will require a computer with high-speed internet connectivity.

Workshop Goal: For workshop attendees to be able to identify a specific process at their organization that would have "collaborative leverage" and understand which collaborative tools and interpersonal techniques to apply to this process to make it a successful pilot project.

Specific Learning Objectives:

1. Understanding the history and development of virtual communication.

2. Knowing available tools and choices for collaboration over time and space.

3. Hands-on understanding of: blogs, wikis, online communities, virtual team spaces, 3-D collaborative environments, social networks, web conferences, screen sharing, application sharing, etc.

4. Understanding the challenges of virtual communication, coordination, and collaboration.

5. Benchmark your group, department, or enterprise on collaboration.

6. Learn what the right collaboration tools are for the right types of conversations.

7. Understanding the real costs of miscommunication and conflict.

8. Understanding the value of effective communication.

9. Understanding the challenge of building high performance teams in a "general's" world.

10. Building an interpersonal communication skills toolbox for the virtual world.

11. Developing beginner's competence in crafting "Agreements for Results."

12. Developing beginner's competence using the "Cycle of Resolution" as a tool for overcoming communication challenges.

1. Introduction

- The Technologies of Trust: Why the Focus on Tools?

- Holistic Approach: People, Process and Technology

- High-Performance Teams Defined

- Successful Holistic Collaboration Defined

- Virtual Collaboration Defined

- 10 Trends in Collaboration

- Looking for Critical Processes with Collaborative Leverage

- First-, Second- and Third-Order Effects of Technology

- Case Studies and Examples

2. Background: The Evolution of Electronic Collaboration

- The Evolution of Communication to Collaboration

- Collaboration 1.0 – What is it? What technologies does it use and where is it today? Why the focus on Content?

- Collaboration 2.0 – What should we expect from these technologies? How do we migrate from Collaboration 1.0? Now the focus is on people and content.

- What are some of the rules and behaviors for Web 2.0?

- Collaboration 2.5 – What to expect in the future? How will we collaborate in virtual worlds?

- What are 3-D Collaborative Environments?

- What are some of the best practices for communicating, coordinating and collaborating in these new virtual environments?

3. Enterprise 2.0

- Definitions: Where Are We Today? How You Can Participate?

- You as a Software Hero: Self-service and Open Source

- SaaS and Security

- E-mail and Collaboration

- Mobile Mail (Push Mail)

4. Best Practices in Collaboration

- 10 Rules for Collaborative Success

- 5 Stages of Collaborative Evolution in the Enterprise

- 10 Steps to Upgrade your Organization in Collaboration

- Looking at VTS and Team Rooms (eRoom, WebEx Office, etc.)

- Questions to Ask Before Using a VTS or Team Room

5. Team Tools and Techniques

- Looking at Web-based Project Tools (Skire, Projity, etc.)
- Looking at Social Networks
- Social Network Analysis
- Value Network Analysis
- The Changing Work Environment
- The Importance of Place

6. Team Productivity and Team Challenges in the Virtual World

- Looking at Different Types of Teams
- The "50-Foot Rule"
- Why Teams Fail (12 Reasons)
- Teaming Challenges

7. Critical Elements of Human Communication

- Delivering Messages in a Collaboration 2.0 Environment
- Receiving Messages in a Collaboration 2.0 Environment
- Building Bridges in a Collaboration 2.0 Environment
- Creating Engagement, Shared Meaning, and Context
- Communication Roadblocks
- The Conflict Continuum

8. Interpersonal Communication Tools

- Moving Through Roadblocks
- No Difficult People – Only Different People
- Instruments Demonstrate Differences
- Developing Emotional Intelligence

- Responding and Reacting

- Anger and Aggression

- Passive / Aggressive / Assertive

- "I" Statements

- Know / Do / Feel

- S O F T E N

- Mirroring / Identifying

- Don' t Bark Back at Barking Dogs

- Listening Skills

- Object / Subject

- Goal "Agreements for Results"

- Non-Verbal

- Automatic Writing

- Providing Effective Feedback

- Delegating Effectively

- Becoming a Conscious Communicator

9. Resolutionary Thinking

- Laws and Principles

- The Attitude of Resolution

- Your Attitude to Conflict

- Using Conversational Models

10. Creating Agreements for Results

- 10 Essential Elements of Effective Agreements

- Using as a Project Management Tool

11. The Cycle of Resolution

- Key Definitions
    - Differences
    - Conflict
    - Agreement
    - Resolution
- Four Costs of Conflict
- Causes of Conflict
- Conflict Continuum
- 7 Stages of Conflict Resolution
- 3 Dialogue Steps to Resolution
- Resolutionary Pledge

12. Summary, Discussion, Dialogue

- Looking at Candidate Processes
- Determining Where Collaborative Leverage Could Be Applied
- Is This a Critical Process?
- How Many People Are Involved?
- What is the Current Pain Around the Process?
- What is the Communications Style Currently in the Process?
- Where are Conflicts in the Process?
- What is the Level of Collaboration in Your Culture?

About the Authors

David Coleman, Founder and Managing Director of Collaborative Strategies (http://www.collaborate.com) has been involved with groupware, collaborative technologies, knowledge management (KM), online communities, and social networks since 1989. He is a thought leader, frequent public speaker, industry analyst, and author of books and magazine articles on these topics. His comments and analysis are most frequently found in the "Collaboration Blog." He has worked with a wide range of collaboration vendors including IBM/Lotus, Microsoft, Macromedia, Adobe, Intuit, EMC, and Oracle, and helped them with strategy, positioning, or demand generation projects. He also works with end-user organizations to help them select collaboration technologies, and most recently has been working with them on "collaborative consolidation" within the enterprise, building online communities and creating a variety of social networks. David also works with distributed teams (across organizational boundaries) to make them high-performance teams. He can be reached at: davidc@collaborate.com or at (415) 282-9197.

Stewart Levine is a "Resolutionary." His innovative work with "Agreements for Results" and his "Cycle of Resolution" are unique. *Getting to Resolution: Turning Conflict into Collaboration* was an Executive Book Club Selection; featured by Executive Book Summaries; named one of the 30 Best Business Books of 1998; and called "*a marvelous book*" by Dr. Stephen Covey. It has been translated into Russian, Hebrew. and Portuguese. *The Book of Agreement* has been endorsed by many thought leaders; called "*more practical*" than the classic *Getting to Yes*; and it was named one of the best books of 2003 by CEO Refresher (http://www.Refresher.com). He consults for many government agencies, Fortune 500 companies, professional associations, and organizations of all sizes. He teaches communication and collaboration skills for the American Management Association. You can find more information about him at http://www.Resolution-Works.com. You can reach him at: ResolutionWorks@msn.com or (510) 777-1166.

Index

A

abundance 176, 177
action teams 132
active listening 165
Adobe 40, 47, 73, 81, 108, 117
aggression 153, 158, 161
agreement 150, 172, 178, 195,
    201–210
Agreements for Results 19–21, 168,
    211–220
AJAX (Asynchronous JavaScript and
    XML) 72, 93, 267
Amazon.com 72, 76
America Online (AOL) 40
Android 54–55
Architecture, Engineering, and
    Construction (AEC) 59
assertive behavior 18, 162, 281
asynchronous collaboration 18, 27,
    31, 33, 42–46, 87
audio conferencing 34, 228, 250
augmented environments 12, 84,
    125–127
avatars 26, 105, 108–127
Avistar 38, 39, 251

B

balance techniques 154
Berrett-Koehler 20, 148, 176, 193,
    222
blogs 45–46, 53, 69, 77, 108, 278

C

Calgoo 105
cell phones 62–64

Charles River Quick Start
    program 76
Cisco 35, 37, 40, 47, 49, 121
cognitive conflicts 136
collaboration
    3-D 111–129
    benefits 19, 25, 190, 235, 247
    definition 17–18
    essential elements 213–218
    problems 95, 179, 199
    recommendations for
        success 244
    trends 33–66
Collaboration 1.0 83–92, 94
Collaboration 2.0 93–105, 145–148,
    199
Collaboration 2.5 107–129
Collaboration 3.0 91
collaborative environments
    115–129, 232
collaborative leverage 51, 142, 233
collaborative pain 24, 236
Collaborative Strategies (CS) 17, 42,
    53, 76, 99, 227
collaborative technologies 26–32,
    69–71, 228–246
communication 66, 132, 145–155
communication roadblocks 149–152
Communication Toolbox 157–170
communities
    online 140
    types of 78
community tools 77
conferencing 27, 34, 228, 250
conflict 136, 153–155
connection 75, 162
conscious communicator 155, 172

roles 215, 219

S

T

U

V

W

Web 1.0 30, 31, 84, 85, 90
Web 1.0-4.0 83—92
Web 2.0 5, 9, 30, 31, 84, 85, 90
Web 3.0 83, 84, 90, 107, 127
Web3D consortium 114
WebEx 34, 37, 42, 47, 53
Wikipedia 43, 44, 72, 84
wikis 31, 43—45, 53
Windows Vista 49
Wonderland 122—125
World Wide Web 90
WYSIWYG editing 44

X

X3D shared file format 114

Y

Yahoo! 74, 91, 108
Yahoo! Messenger 40
YouTube 69, 75, 85

Z

Zimbra 40, 49, 56, 58, 61

Create Thought Leadership for Your Company

Books deliver instant credibility to the author. Having an MBA or PhD is great, however, putting the word "author" in front of your name is similar to using the letters PhD or MBA. You are no long Michael Green, you are "Author Michael Green."

Books give you a platform to stand on. They help you to:

- Demonstrate your thought leadership
- Generate leads

Books deliver increased revenue, particularly indirect revenue:

- A typical consultant will make 3x in indirect revenue for every dollar they make on book sales

Books are better than a business card. They are:

- More powerful than white papers
- An item that makes it to the book shelf vs. the circular file
- The best tchotchke you can give at a conference

Why wait to write your book?

Check out other companies that have built credibility by writing and publishing a book through Happy About

Contact Happy About at 408-257-3000 or go to http://happyabout.info.

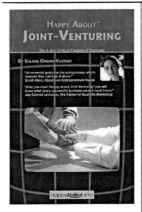
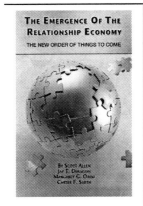

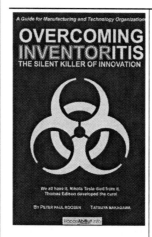

Printed in the United Kingdom
by Lightning Source UK Ltd.
129547UK00001B/25/A